DEFENDING YOUR *Faith*

A Twelve Lesson Series
on Apologetics

DR. MARK BIRD

LEADER'S GUIDE

1:1
answersingenesis
Hebron, Kentucky
United States of America

D1253149

Acknowledgements

I would especially like to express my appreciation to Josh McDowell for his contribution to this book. His materials provided a basis for much of what is taught in the following pages. Of course, many others have contributed to this work as it has been developed over the years. Many other authors' works have been consulted, many people have reviewed the work (including my college Apologetics classes), and several have taught the course and have offered feedback. To all, I give my thanks.

Second printing: January 2007

Copyright © 2006 Mark Bird. All rights reserved. No part of this book may be used or reproduced in any manner whatsoever without the written permission from the publisher. For more information write: Answers in Genesis, PO Box 510, Hebron KY 41048.

ISBN: 1-60092-016-0

Cover design: Ingrid Beyer & Tommy Moore
Interior layout: Diane King
Editor: Gary Vaterlaus

All Scripture quotations are taken from the New King James Version. Copyright © 1982 by Thomas Nelson, Inc. Used by permission. All rights reserved.

Printed in the United States of America

CONTENTS

FOREWORD

BY KEN HAM

PRESIDENT OF ANSWERS IN GENESIS AND THE CREATION MUSEUM

*I*t's very sad every time it happens. My heart breaks whenever parents approach me at an AiG seminar and—often with moist eyes—tell me how their son or daughter "gave up" their Christian faith while in school.

This kind of confession usually comes after I've given a talk on the authority of the Bible, and how churches have generally done a poor job in equipping their congregations to defend their faith and show that the Bible truly is God's reliable Word. The parents see how this lapse has led their child to leave church and reject the Christian faith.

In 2006 our AiG ministry conducted a national poll of 1,000 Americans who are now in their 20s who once regularly attended an evangelical church but no longer do. One of the striking findings was that, in addition to these young adults finding church to be largely irrelevant, a sizeable number (70%) told surveyors they wonder if the Bible contains errors. Their doubts about the Bible became most acute while in high school, which is not all that surprising, for this is a time when one would think that topics challenging the Bible (like evolution and millions of years) would be more likely to be brought up in class.

This poll certainly reveals a crisis in the church. It is a crisis that must be increasingly addressed by leaders in the church. Apologetics ministries, such as AiG, can only do so much in addressing this mammoth problem of Bible-doubting, and so we are encouraged to know that there are resources like Mark Bird's new book that we are happy to be co-publishing.

This practical book by Dr. Bird will equip church leaders to counter the anti-Christian indoctrination that so many young people in our churches are getting in most public schools.

While it's encouraging to see more people being interested in pressuring school boards to see that anti-Bible teaching (e.g., evolution) is minimized, there is so much more that can be done. These things should be done at a grassroots level to ensure that our young people won't leave the church because of what they learned in school (or in other places, like the media, science documentaries, etc.).

Conversely, we are seeing many more evolutionists becoming more aggressive in indoctrinating young people in the worldview of evolutionary humanism. It is my contention that evolutionists are desperately concerned by the fact that the biblical creation movement continues to make major inroads around the country.

The high priests of the worldwide faith known as "evolution" are so concerned, in fact, that museums are allocating millions of more dollars (much of it your tax dollars) to beef up their evolutionary exhibits. Also, we are already

5

seeing that secular educators are teaching evolution with even more intensity. Secularists are on an aggressive crusade—and most science instructors have joined them—to teach children (and adults) that they are descended from animals in a purposeless existence.

Biblical Christians need to "take back" our students and teach them that they are made in the image of God, not the image of an ape. They must teach young people that: 1) the infinite God of creation stepped into history to pay the penalty for their sin so they can spend eternity with Him in Heaven, and 2) the Bible's account of history (and thus the gospel message itself) is true.

To this end, apologetics ministries and new resources like this book are being raised up by the Lord to help parents (and other godly teachers) to accomplish what was done for godly Timothy:

"… that from a child thou hast known the holy scriptures, which are able to make thee wise unto salvation through faith which is in Christ Jesus" (2 Timothy 3:15).

One way to assist students to counter the religion of humanism in schools is to help them understand that true science confirms the creation account in Genesis and that molecules-to-man evolution is a blind-faith belief that flies in the face of much scientific evidence.

This new book by Mark Bird, even though it is not designed for use by a public school class (although teachers should read it to see the nature of the battle in the schools), can be a mighty tool in equipping church-going students to be confirmed in their belief in biblical authority, and to equip them to give answers for their faith.

Dr. Bird's text features useful information that will help students defend their precious faith. Students need to know how to answer tough questions like:

> If there's a God of love, why is there so much death and suffering in the world?

> What evidence is there for the Resurrection of Christ?

> How do we know that the Bible has been copied correctly?

I am pleased to see this book join the growing arsenal of resources that will equip the church to restore biblical authority beginning with Genesis. Then and only then, with God's blessing, will the secular worldview that is so dominant in society (and particularly in its schools) be successfully counteracted. Our young people need to be rescued as quickly as possible before they turn their backs on the church forever.

Read … and become ready, to reach your young people before it's too late.

BEFORE YOU GET STARTED

*A*re you ready to help your students learn to defend their faith? There are two reasons you should consider teaching this course in your Wednesday night adult Bible study, small group Bible study, Sunday School class, or high school Bible class: 1) Christians need to be equipped in the area of apologetics; 2) This course has been developed using the "Laws of the Learner," a set of teaching principles and methods that help teachers make lessons interesting and equipping. The lessons in this series are designed to effectively and creatively equip Christians to defend their faith.

CHRISTIANS NEED TRAINING TO DEFEND THEIR FAITH

It is becoming increasingly important in this age of pluralism and secularism for Christians to be equipped in the discipline of apologetics.

What is apologetics? Apologetics is the rational defense of one's faith. It is giving reasons for what one believes. Christian apologetics presents evidences and rational arguments to someone who doubts the truth of Christianity or to someone who wants better reasons for believing that the Bible is true and Christianity is the only valid religion.

Apologetics comes from the Greek word *apologia*, which means "defense." In ancient Greece, a defendant on trial would give his *apologia* after being accused by the prosecution. In the same way, Christians give an *apologia* when the truth of Christianity is attacked by non-Christians. Apologetics needs to be distinguished from polemics, since many people tend to confuse the two. Polemics deals with attacks on biblical Christianity from within the church. Polemics happens when Christians fight erroneous doctrine that comes from people who claim to be orthodox Christians.

Polemics often relates to "secondary issues," though not always. Apologetics defends the *major* tenets of Christian theology from attacks on the "outside."

A believer should learn apologetics: 1) To strengthen his faith, and 2) To help him share his faith. Christians will be strengthened spiritually when they are shown that their faith is reasonable and supported by historical and scientific evidence. When a Christian is strong in faith and properly equipped, he can go out to be successful in "giving an answer to those who ask" (1 Peter 3:15). We should present evidences for Christianity to non-believers because removing intellectual obstacles may move them one step closer to the Cross (and a commitment to Christ). Apologetics gives the unbeliever sufficient reasons for accepting the gospel.

1 Peter 3:15 admonishes Christians to be always ready to give a defense to everyone who asks for a reason for the hope within them. As the church obeys the command to "equip the saints for the work of the ministry" (Ephesians 4:11, 12), she must be preparing Christians to defend the basic truths of Christianity. Preparation for the defense of the faith is part of the church's job to "equip the saints." Therefore, the Sunday school teacher or Bible teacher is legitimately considered responsible to help his or her students strengthen and defend their faith.

As I said at the beginning of this Introduction, the second reason that one might consider teaching this course is that it was developed using the "Laws of the Learner." In the following paragraphs, I will describe the book *The 7 Laws of the Learner*, and discuss the laws that were applied to the course in order to make the course effective.

THE LAWS OF THE LEARNER

Dr. Bruce Wilkinson has revolutionized the way students respond to some teachers. These are the teachers who apply the principles in his book *The 7 Laws of the Learner*.[1] These biblically-based "Laws of the Learner" enable teachers to teach for life change. The Laws not only help teachers at school and Sunday school, but also parents at home, employers at work, and pastors in the pulpit. The Laws show someone "how to teach almost anything to practically anyone." The Laws will help the person who fully applies them become a master communicator.

The Laws of the Learner are built on the thesis that the teacher is responsible for the education of the student. If a student hasn't learned, then the teacher hasn't taught. A teacher is responsible because he has control over the three primary relationships that directly impact most classroom situations: his relationship to the student, the subject, and his style.[2]

There are three of the 7 Laws of the Learner that are most relevant to a course on apologetics. They are the "Law of Need," the "Law of Retention," and the "Law of Equipping."

THE LAW OF NEED

The "Law of Need" will enable the teacher to create a classroom environment where the students are begging to hear what the instructor has to say, where the students are disappointed when class is over, where the word "boring" is never used—because the teacher isn't boring.

The "Law of Need" states that the teacher is responsible for "need building," or for awakening the interest of the student. Need *meeting* is the teacher's primary calling. Therefore, it is the responsibility of the teacher to *discover* the true needs of the students, then to *awaken* the realization of the need in the minds of the students, so that finally the teacher can *satisfy* their need.

Need building is the teacher's main method to motivate students. The teacher must "bait the hook" if he is going to have motivated students. The "bait" will be effective in motivating students to the degree that it is felt. The teacher must touch the students' feelings. In order to arouse the feelings of the students, helping them desire the content of the lesson, the "need building" teacher will use the seven universal motivators.

The seven motivators that will help the students "feel the need," and thus be interested in what the teacher has to say, are: 1) A factual presentation that is shocking, totally unexpected, or presented in such a way that the listener sees the facts from a new perspective; 2) Storytelling; 3) Drama; 4) The teacher's delivery (use of voice, eyes, hands, and body—intensity is the key); 5) Music; 6) Diagrams; 7) Pictures.[3] All these motivators build the need

to the extent that they touch the emotions of the students.

THE LAW OF RETENTION

In presenting the "Law of Retention," Wilkinson claims that minimal mastery of this law will enable a teacher to cause a student to memorize twice the material in half the time.[4] Teachers will "speed teach" not just any facts, but the most important facts of any subject. The "Law of Retention" states that it is the responsibility of the teacher to cause the students to "master the minimum;" that is, to know and use the most important facts or concepts. The following three principles accompany the "Law of Retention": 1) Retention of facts is effective only after they are understood; 2) retention increases as the student recognizes the content's relevance; and 3) the teacher must focus on the most important facts, and then use regular review in order to strengthen long-term memory of these facts.[5]

This law rejects the standard procedure of teachers dumping vast amounts of content onto the students without the students knowing for sure what is most important. The law says that the teacher must be very selective in what he chooses to present. He should generally only present the most important facts. Once selecting the facts, the teacher must take the time to arrange the content in a way that is easy to memorize; then, in class, he must help the students memorize the material. The student's time outside class should not be used for memorization but for application of what Wilkinson calls the "irreducible minimum."

The five step method by which a teacher can help the students master the "irreducible minimum" is: *Before class,* 1) Gather the material by overviewing the subject, organizing the subject, and finally outlining the subject. 2) Out of all the material surveyed, identify the irreducible minimum (the most important concepts to master). 3) Restructure (or package) the material in such a way that the irreducible minimum is "easy on the mind" ("mindeasy") and thus easy to remember. *In class* 4) Help the students to memorize the "memorizable" irreducible minimum. In this step the teacher reviews the content with the students enough for the material to move from short-term memory to long-term memory. 5) Help the students "master the minimum." In this step the students become skillful in the use of the material they memorized by applying it outside class.[6]

The five steps of the Retention method can be summarized in five words: Material, Minimum, Mindeasy, Memorize, Master.

The third step, Mindeasy, can be a challenge to the inexperienced teacher. But Wilkinson helps by listing specific ways the teacher can package the material for ease of memorization. The teacher causes the student to remember the material by using pictures, stories, the alphabet (for instance, arranging the points on the outline in an acrostic, or doing what Wilkinson does by starting each Retention step with an "M"), drama, music, graphs and charts, and/or objects and actions.[7]

THE LAW OF EQUIPPING

The "Law of Equipping" states that equipping is the responsibility of the Christian teacher. According to Ephesians 4:11–12, teachers are a gift of God to the church to help equip the saints for ministry. Teachers are not simply dispensers of information, but equipping agents. Ultimately, the teacher should reproduce himself in the skills that he is teaching his students. It is not enough to inform or entertain students. The primary purpose of teachers is to equip.[8]

Sunday school teachers must move their focus from the lesson that was taught to the ministry done after class. Teachers must do more to train students to be effective in ministry activities.

The common practice of most teachers, employers, pastors, and parents is to instruct someone in a certain activity or skill, and then, using a lot of guilt and exhortation, attempt to motivate them to participate in the activity. This approach does not usually succeed. The "Law of Equipping" says that teachers must not skip any steps in the equipping process. Certain steps in the equipping process should be used in any place, for any teacher, with any student, and for any skill. They are universal. They work equally well for teaching someone to ride a horse or to witness. These five steps (The Equipping Method) are:

1. Instruct (*Tell* them how to do something);

2. Illustrate (*Show* them how to do something—give them a live preview);

3. Involve (Have the students participate in the process—they are doing the skill *with* you);

4. Improve (Have the students do something *on their own*, then critique);

5. Inspire (*Encourage* the students to continue to use the skill and pass it on).[9]

These laws were applied to this course on apologetics in an attempt to make the course interesting and effective in equipping Christians to defend their faith.

CONTENT OF APOLOGETICS COURSE

This course on apologetics discusses the following: the existence of God, evidence for biblical Creation and against evolution, historical reliability of the New Testament, Resurrection of Christ, prophecies of Christ, deity of Christ, and inspiration of Scripture. These topics are included because of their importance to a compelling case for Christianity. We start with the existence of God. Belief in the existence of God is foundational to other Christian beliefs. Since the belief in evolution is a popular alternative to a belief in God, we spend a couple of lessons arguing for creation and against evolution. Then we discuss the historical reliability of the New Testament. If we can demonstrate that the N.T. can be trusted historically, we can have reasonable assurance that Jesus rose from the dead and fulfilled dozens of Messianic prophecies. If the fulfillment of prophecy and the Resurrection are true, then we have confidence that Jesus is who He said He was—God in the flesh. If Jesus is God, then we can trust His testimony that the Bible is the very Word of God and that He is the only way to Heaven.

Central to this course is the following argument, which assumes belief in a divine Creator. In syllogistic form:

Is the Bible the Word of God and Jesus the Only Way to Heaven?

Premise A: The New Testament is historically accurate; it is a basically reliable and trustworthy document.

Premise B: We have sufficient evidence from this reliable document to believe that Jesus rose from the dead as He predicted He would and that He fulfilled dozens of other Messianic prophecies.

Premise C: Jesus' Resurrection and fulfillment of prophecy show that He is who He said He was: the Messiah, the Son of God—God in the flesh.

Premise D: As the Son of God (God the Son), Jesus Christ is an infallible authority—what He says is absolutely trustworthy.

Premise E: Jesus Christ taught that the Bible was the Word of God (Matt. 5:18, 15:4; Mark 12:36; Luke 24:44–46). He also taught that He was the only way to God (John 14:6).

Conclusion: If Christ said it, we must believe it—the Bible is the Word of God, and Jesus is the only way to God.

Each of the above premises needs to be demonstrated to be true before we can be certain of the final conclusion. The apologetics lessons try to substantiate each of the above premises so that one comes to the conclusion that the Bible is the divinely inspired Word of God and that Jesus is the only way to God.

Substantiating the above premises necessitates a discussion of the historical reliability of the New Testament, the Resurrection of Christ, fulfilled Messianic prophecies, and the deity of Christ. Each of these is not only important to our argument for Christianity, but they were also important to the Bible writers. For instance, Luke makes it clear that the things he was writing were accurate (Luke 1:1–4). This suggests a concern for historical reliability. Paul argued that Jesus rose from the dead and fulfilled Messianic prophecies (Acts 17). John said that he wrote his gospel in order to show that Jesus was the Son of God—God the Son (John 20:31). Almost the whole first chapter of Hebrews argues against any belief which makes Christ a being inferior to God. These doctrines that were important to the Bible writers are defended in this course.

HISTORICAL RELIABILITY OF THE NEW TESTAMENT

A great deal of emphasis is placed on the historical reliability of the New Testament. Without a reliable New Testament, we have no reason to believe in the Resurrection, fulfilled prophecy, or the deity of Christ. Fortunately, there is available to us a vast amount of *objective* evidence in favor of a historically accurate New Testament. A significant portion of the course is devoted to presenting some of that evidence.

THE RESURRECTION OF JESUS

According to I Corinthians 15, if Christ did not resurrect bodily (in time and space) from the dead, then the faith of the Christian is in vain. Christianity becomes meaningless. It is therefore important that Christians not only affirm the fact of the Resurrection, but also support their belief in the Resurrection with strong historical evidence.

What does the Resurrection prove? Jesus' predicted death and Resurrection were the sign that Jesus gave to the unbelieving Jews to confirm that He was who He claimed to be. Historical evidence that Jesus rose from the dead will confirm our faith that Jesus was God and therefore is absolutely trustworthy in His words. For this reason we have a lengthy lesson discussing the Resurrection.

Another major reason this course discusses the Resurrection is that one of the marks of a true Christian is his affirmation of the bodily Resurrection of Jesus from the dead. No one who denies the Resurrection can become a Christian. A person must believe the gospel in order to be saved. What is the gospel? It is that Christ (the God-man) died for our sins, was buried, and was raised from the dead (1 Corinthians 15:3–4). Romans 10:9 says that in order for a person to be saved, he must believe in his heart that Jesus rose from the dead. The doctrine of the Resurrection is therefore crucial to Christianity and must be defended.

FULFILLED MESSIANIC PROPHECIES

The prophecies that Jesus fulfilled are discussed because they identify Jesus as the predicted Messiah. Jesus Himself appealed to those prophecies as evidence that He was the Christ. The apostles (such as Matthew and Paul) also refer to Messianic prophecies when they present their case for Jesus as the Messiah. The fulfilled prophecies not only substantiate Jesus' claim to be the Messiah, but also demonstrate that Jesus, being the Christ, was also God—since the Messiah was to be a divine Person.10

THE DEITY OF CHRIST

We defend the deity of Christ because of the crucial nature of the doctrine. Jesus said that unless one believed that "I Am," he would die in his sins (John 8:24). Jesus was identifying himself with Jehovah, the I AM of the Old Testament. If Jesus claims to be God, and says that we must believe this in order to be saved, then it is extremely important that we defend this doctrine.

It would be hard to overemphasize the importance of the doctrine of the deity of Christ. Only one who is both God and man could accomplish redemption. If Jesus were not God, He could not have atoned for our sins. The sacrifice for sins must have been an infinite sacrifice to be worthy to atone for the sins of the whole world against an infinite God. The only one who can save is the God-man. A person who professes to believe in Jesus while refusing to believe that He is God is believing in a "Jesus" who cannot save anyone. A person who refuses to acknowledge Jesus as Lord and God cannot be saved because one can exercise true saving faith only in a Person with the power to save.

This course also defends the deity of Christ in order to show that His words can be trusted absolutely. If we can affirm Christ's absolute trustworthiness (since He is divine), then we have no reason to doubt His assertions that the Bible is inspired of God and that He is the only way to Heaven. This actually is part of this course's general argument for Christianity.

INSTRUCTIONS

Make sure that you are careful to follow the instructions in the lessons. You should read through each lesson weeks before you plan to teach it to make sure you are able to get any props or materials that will help the class be more effective. The activities and visuals are part of the application of the Laws of the Learner.

You will notice text boxes scattered throughout the lessons. In these boxes, I explain how the Laws of the Learner are applied. Obviously, you will not share the content of the boxes with the students; they are for you to read in preparation. It will remind you of the importance of using the methods suggested, rather than simply presenting the material.

Each student should have a student workbook where they will take notes, fill in the blanks, and be able to follow the lessons. At the back of this book, you will find supplemental material such as quizzes, illustrations, or charts. These could simply be held up so the students can see them as you discuss them, or you may use the PowerPoint presentation of this course, which is available for download from the Answers in Genesis website at www.answersingenesis.org/go/defending-your-faith. The student workbook is also available for downloading in PDF format, or you may purchase it separately from Answers in Genesis.

Something probably needs to be said concerning the age-level of the curriculum. The material and activities should be appropriate for teens and adults. However, older adults may not feel comfortable with a few of the activities.

In Lesson Six, you are instructed to use wooden blocks to literally build a case for Christianity. These blocks are very important to the success of the course. To make the blocks, simply cut a 2x4 into six pieces of equal length (about 16 inches per piece). Then use a black marker to write the appropriate phrases on the blocks.

It would be most helpful (almost necessary if you have not recently read some good apologetics books) for you to read the book, *The Case for Christ*, by Lee Strobel, in preparation to teach this course.[11] You may also want to have your students read the book as you work through the lessons. It is an excellent supplemental text. Listed at the back of this book are other apologetics resources that you may want to get as well.

PAGE FORMAT

The lessons have been designed with a two-column format. The left column is what the students will see in their notes, while the right column is for the teacher. (Please note that the words in brackets, in the left column, are to be filled in by the student and do not appear in their notes.) The sentences **in bold** are to be read to the students, as are the student notes in the left column. You will move back and forth between the columns as you teach through the lessons.

The words and phrases in ALL CAPS should be written on the marker board. Instructions to the teacher are {within ellipticals}. The sentences enclosed in boxes tell how the Laws of the Learner are used in the lesson. These Laws-of-the-Learner boxes, as well as the illustrations, may occur in the left or right column, as space allows.

Become very familiar with the words in bold; try to make them your own, so that when you present the lesson you can come very close to the language of the text without being tied to the notes. This will mean lots of practice. It is recommended that you read the text out loud several times before presenting it in public or deciding to change or eliminate something.

If you have any questions about this course, feel free to email the author, Mark Bird, at MBird777@aol.com. After you have taught this course, please send feedback to the same email address. Feel free to offer suggestions for improvements.

NOTES

[1] Bruce Wilkinson, *The 7 Laws of the Learner*, Multnomah Press, Sisters, OR, 1992). Our endorsement of the teaching methods outlined in this book by Dr. Wilkinson does not mean that we endorse all of his teachings or other writings.
[2] Ibid., 48–50.
[3] Ibid., 269–276.
[4] Ibid., 189.
[5] Ibid.,180–189.
[6] Ibid.,197–209.
[7] Ibid., 210–218.
[8] Ibid., 287.
[9] Ibid., 315–322.
[10] Isaiah 9:6; Psalm 110:1.
[11] Lee Strobel, *The Case for Christ*, Zondervan, Grand Rapids, 1998.

1 INTRODUCTION TO APOLOGETICS

I. WHAT IS APOLOGETICS?

{Read the instructions on pages 13 and 14 before beginning.}

{Have the word APOLOGETICS written on the board. To begin class you might use a little drama: two of your students will dramatically apologize to each other in front of class.}

The topic we are discussing this quarter is apologetics. We are going to learn how to give an apologetic for Christianity. Is the apologizing we just saw up here what this class on apologetics is all about? Will we learn how to do that kind of apologizing?

{wait for answer}

No, actually the word *apology* has two meanings. We usually use the word *apology* to mean that we're sorry for something, but this meaning originally was only a secondary meaning of the word. This class is about the *other* meaning of *apology*. How would you define apologetics the way we are using it in this class?

{Wait 3–5 seconds to see if anyone can answer. Remember that the words in ALL CAPS are to be written on the board.}

It is the **DEFENSE OF THE FAITH**; giving reasons for what you believe; Christian apologetics is **PRESENTING THE EVIDENCE FOR THE VALIDITY OF CHRISTIANITY.**

{Have students memorize the definitions on the board. Have them say the definitions twice in unison after writing them down, once while looking at their notes, and once looking up from their notes.}

THE LAWS OF THE LEARNER APPLIED:

The "apologizing" at the beginning of the lesson is an attention-getter. It will help build the need for knowing about apologetics. The story that Kennedy tells and the "Reality Card" (with the subsequent questions) will build the need for becoming equipped to defend the faith. The objection brought up by the Reality Card will be answered later in the course. Bringing up the question now will build the need for the later answer. The Law of Retention is used when the definitions of apologetics are repeated.

D. James Kennedy was motivated to write a book on apologetics after hearing a radio talk show. The host had been interviewing an atheist. Kennedy testifies, "While frantically trying to get a call through to the station, I listened to a dozen or more Christian callers talk to this man. I was appalled at the ease with which he was chewing them up and spitting them out. It seemed that every Christian who called was incapable of giving an intelligent reason for the faith that he or she held. 'The Bible says such and such,' each would begin in trying to support what he was saying. The atheist would counter: 'Well, why do you believe the Bible?' Every one of them was reduced to stammering out something like, 'Well, I've got it down in my heart.' The atheist would answer, 'Well, it's not down in my heart, friend, and I don't believe it.'"[1]

Would you have had an answer for the atheist?

On the internet, there used to be a website called "Stump the Bible Thumpers." The website advertised a "Reality Card" that attacked the credibility of the Bible with 10 questions that are supposedly impossible to answer. Non-Christians were encouraged to buy this card and stump Christians by asking them the questions on the card.

One of the questions was, "If the Bible is the unchangeable Word of God, why does Mark 15:25 state Jesus was crucified the third hour (9:00 a.m.) while John 19:14 states it was the

sixth hour (12:00 p.m.)?" Could you respond to this objection to the Bible's accuracy?

If someone were to present to you a card like this, would you be afraid to read it for fear that maybe someone found some real problems in the Bible?

II. WHY STUDY APOLOGETICS?

Based on what I just shared with you, do you think it is important to be able to defend our faith? Why do you think we should study apologetics?

{Wait for answers, then suggest the following reasons.}

It helps in PRE-EVANGELISM and in POST-EVANGELISM. *Pre*-evangelism is what we do to help a person get closer to committing his life to Christ. A Christian can use apologetics to remove intellectual obstacles in the path of someone on his way to faith. *Post*-evangelism is what we do to help Christians become strengthened in their faith after they are converted.

Why is apologetics important in *pre*-evangelism? Because many people have come to know Christ after studying the evidence for the validity of Christianity. C. S. Lewis was at one time an atheist who reluctantly became a Christian after discovering that Christianity was true. Speaking of the time he was an atheist, C. S. Lewis said, "I thought I had the Christians … disposed of forever." But "a young man who wishes to remain a sound atheist cannot be too careful of his reading. There are traps everywhere—'Bible laid open, millions of surprises,' as Herbert says, 'Fine nets and stratagems.' God is, if I may say it, very unscrupulous." The evidence for Christianity that Lewis saw was so compelling that he could not escape it, even though he wanted to. He said that he was brought in "kicking, struggling, resentful, and darting [his] eyes in every direction for a chance of escape." Of course, later he was glad he became a Christian. He titled his story, *Surprised by Joy*.

Josh McDowell was also a skeptic who converted to Christianity after studying apologetics. He tried to disprove Christianity, but all the evidence pointed toward the truth of Christianity, so he became a Christian. He wrote the book *Evidence that Demands a Verdict*.

Lee Strobel, author of *Case for Christ*, was an atheist who became a Christian after studying the evidence for Christianity. One of the books he read was *Evidence that Demands a Verdict*.

{If you have these books, show them to the class.}

Apologetics is an effective pre-evangelism tool. If you present apologetics to someone who is not sure that Christianity is true, you may remove an intellectual stumbling block that is keeping him from believing the gospel. *Apologetics helps you to remove the intellectual roadblocks on a person's road to the Cross.*

{Have the student's write down the previous sentence that is in italics. Illustrate this on the board, drawing a stick figure, a path, a cross, and huge stones representing intellectual obstacles.}

In this way, apologetics will help you SHARE YOUR FAITH.

As I said earlier, apologetics also helps in *post-evangelism*.

{Point to the word on the board.}

It will not only help you *share* your faith, but it will also STRENGTHEN YOUR FAITH and the faith of others. This is post-evangelism. Knowing why you believe what you believe will make you strong in The Faith.

Did you know that about 40% of those who identify themselves as born-again Christians think that it doesn't matter what religion you belong to because all faiths teach similar lessons about life? Statistics like that demonstrate that

Christians do not know why they believe what they believe, and that they are vulnerable to the faith-destroying attacks of the skeptic.

{If you are teaching a teen class, have secret volunteers interrupt. You have already given them a paper with instructions on exactly what to say. These volunteers will pretend not to have a problem with non-Christian religions.

1st Volunteer: "Wait a minute: I think there are many ways to God. My cousin is into Eastern mysticism, and it's not as weird as some people think."

2nd Volunteer: "I feel that if you really believe it doesn't matter as long as you are sincere."

1st Volunteer: "Yeah, if what you believe in makes you happy, what's the big deal?"[2]}

{Get reactions from other students. Finally tell them that this was a set-up, but that there are a lot of people who believe exactly what they said. These people are vulnerable to the attacks of skeptics.}

{Give other statistics and/or stories about those Christians who lose faith because their faith was undermined. Maybe you could tell a story about someone from a Christian home who went to the university and became first confused, then skeptical because he did not know why he believed what he believed.}

Apologetics will make you more ready to answer the skeptics that try to tear down your faith. What happens if you study apologetics? If you were to listen to a radio talk show like the one we mentioned earlier, you will not become weak in your faith, but you may instead be moved to call the program and show everyone that Christianity *is* defensible.

As your teacher, I use apologetics in a couple ways: outside class time, I use apologetics when I *share my faith*—when I witness to non-Christians, removing some of the obstacles on their way to the Cross. This is *pre-evangelism*.

I also *strengthen your faith* as Christians. This is *post-evangelism*. I also teach you how *you* can, using apologetics, share *your* faith more

---

THE LAWS OF THE LEARNER APPLIED:

The secret volunteers will build the need because of the feelings that will surface when someone in class is perceived as a skeptic. The statistics and stories will build the need as well. Statistics and stories are two of the seven primary ways that a teacher can build need, according to Bruce Wilkinson.

effectively. Some of the non-Christians that you and I talk to will become Christians as we share the gospel and apologetics with them.

Now let's go back to the top to review. Give me two definitions of apologetics. Everyone say the first one without looking at your notes.

{Wait for response.}

What is the second definition?

{Have everyone say this aloud together.}

Why do we say that apologetics is a pre-evangelism activity?

{Call on someone to answer. The correct answer is that we can use apologetics to remove intellectual obstacles on a person's way to the Cross.}

Why do we say that apologetics is also a post-evangelism activity?

{Call on someone else to answer. The correct answer is that through apologetics, we help those who are already Christians know why they believe what they believe. Thus, we strengthen their faith (and ours) and make them less vulnerable to spiritual failure.}

THE LAWS OF THE LEARNER APPLIED:

These review questions accord with *Memorize*, the fourth step of the Retention Method.

III. WHERE IN SCRIPTURE ARE WE COMMANDED TO USE APOLOGETICS?

Actually, the biggest reason we should study and use apologetics is that the Bible tells us that we should be always ready to defend our faith. Where in 1 Peter do we find that command?

{Wait to see if someone can answer. Have students fill in the blank, and then read the verse together.}

1 Peter <u>3:15</u>

"But sanctify the Lord God in your hearts, and always be ready to give a [<u>defense</u>] to everyone who asks you a reason for the hope that is in you, with meekness and fear" (NKJV).

Which word in this verse do you think is translated from the Greek word *apologia*?[3] The Greek word translated "defense" is *apologia*. {Wait for answer.}

Did you know that the word *apologia* was used in ancient Greece to refer to the defense of a person accused in court? The person with the complaint would present his accusation (his *categoria*). Then the accused would give his *apologia* (his defense).

{Have a previously set-up drama in which one student is accused of murder; he goes to court, gets sworn in, then the plaintiff brings the accusation (the *categoria*). The defendant is accused of murder (maybe he is accused of killing his brother at 7:00 p.m. on Christmas Eve.) Then the defendant speaks in his own defense (he gives his *apologia*). He explains why he could not have been the murderer, since he was at a party with some friends at the time of the "accident." You, the teacher, be the judge and let the class be the jury. This activity should take 2–3 minutes.}

What do we call the defense the defendant gave? {Wait for answer.}

He gave an *apologia*. What does *apologia* mean? {Wait for answer.}

Apologia means "defense." 1 Peter 3:15 says we are to be ready to give a defense—a reasoned explanation[4]—to everyone who asks us to give a reason for our hope as Christians. We are to give reasons for our beliefs.

When we give our defense for Christianity, *how* are we to give it (according to the last part of the verse)? {Wait for answer.}

With meekness and fear, or gentleness and respect for everyone we talk to.

Let's recite 1 Peter 3:15 a couple of times.

{Everyone should recite the verse aloud, twice looking at the notes, then twice without looking. Make sure you are leading the recitation from memory. Then have one person quote it.}

THE LAWS OF THE LEARNER APPLIED:

The drama of the word apologia builds the need for apologetics and also helps the students remember the meaning of apologetics. Reciting 1 Peter 3:15 together will also aid memory (Law of Retention).

IV. WHEN SHOULD WE PRESENT APOLOGETICS, BEFORE OR AFTER THE GOSPEL?

THE LAWS OF THE LEARNER APPLIED:

The words on the board and the little diagrams that represent "gospel" and "apologetics" accomplish the *Mindeasy* step of the Retention Method. The diagrams may also help build the need. Using diagrams is one of the seven need-builders according to the 7 Laws of the Learner.

Gospel ⟶

US | GOD

Apologetics

When should we present apologetics? Should we present it before or after we present the gospel? What is the proper timing?

{Take various responses. The students may want to "debate" this one. You may want to bring up different scenarios of evangelism opportunities.}

When you are sharing your faith, present the GOSPEL first, then if necessary fall back onto APOLOGETICS. There will be exceptions to the rule of "gospel first." For instance, sometimes you may want to use an interesting apologetic topic as a launching pad into a discussion of the basic message of the Bible. The important thing for us to remember is that the gospel is primary. Share the gospel. It is the most important thing. Use apologetics if people bring up an objection, or if using apologetics will increase your likelihood to be able to share the gospel.

{Have students write down *Gospel first, then Apologetics*. Next to "Gospel," draw a brief sketch of the gulf that separated man from God and the Cross that bridged the gulf; next to "Apologetics," draw an arrow to the sketch you already drew of the man on the rocky path to the Cross. Explain that these symbolize the gospel and apologetics. Go to page 150 (supplement section) to see a gospel presentation that uses the bridge illustration. Take the earliest possible opportunity to teach this presentation to your students. A PowerPoint of this gospel presentation is available at www.answersingenesis.org/go/defending-your-faith. Show this to the students and have them practice it on each other. Encourage them to share this message with family, friends, neighbors, co-workers and even new acquaintances.}

V. WHO NEEDS APOLOGETICS?

Does every Christian need to know evidence for Christianity?

{Wait 3–5 seconds for answer.}

The answer is "yes." Every Christian needs to know why they believe what they believe at least to an extent. But what about non-Christians? What about those who obviously are non-Christians because they want to be, not because they have an intellectual problem with it?

According to Josh McDowell, people reject Christ for the following reasons:

1) IGNORANCE (many times willful)

2) PRIDE

3) MORAL PROBLEM

{Draw a stick figure for each of these. Just for fun, make the ignorant person with a very tiny head. Make the proud person with a very large head. Give the person with a moral problem a black heart.}

I have met people that have sincere intellectual doubts concerning the truth of Christianity. They are ignorant. These people need apologetics. Other times I have seen people bring up intellectual objections, which are actually excuses to avoid admitting the real reason they don't want to believe—they have sin they do not want to give up, or they are too proud. We need to recognize their real reason for rejecting Christ so we can confront them with it, but this doesn't mean that we don't deal with their intellectual objections. Many times these people will need these intellectual excuses eliminated before they will fully realize the real reason they reject Christ. Since this is the case, anyone who brings up intellectual objections may need to be presented with apologetics, though it is helpful to know the person's main reason for bringing up the objection.

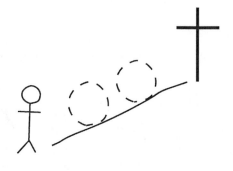

THE LAWS OF THE LEARNER APPLIED:

The little stick figures that represent the proud, sinful, and ignorant persons will help build the need and aid retention. The diagram of the man, path, Cross, and stones (with disconnected lines) will build the need and aid understanding and memory (Law of Retention).

One way to clarify the real issue would be to ask a person if he would become a Christian if his intellectual objections were removed.

{Draw the man, the path, the Cross, and the stones again, but this time make the stones with disconnected lines, representing objections that are more imaginary—they are simply excuses.}

What are three reasons people reject Christ?

{Wait for answer.}

Does someone with a moral problem ever need apologetics?

{Wait for answer.}

Even rebellious or proud people who know the truth may need apologetics at times, even if it's just to eliminate their intellectual excuses.

Let's review from the top. Without looking at your notes, what are two definitions for apologetics? Number one:

{Wait for response. They should all say it together out loud.}

Number two:

{Wait for response.}

How will apologetics help us as Christians?

{Wait for responses. Get at least two.}

Let's all recite 1 Peter 3:15. Ready?

{Quote verse together.}

What does the word *apologia* mean?

{Wait for answer.}

What comes first, apologetics or the gospel?

{Call on someone to answer.}

What are the three reasons people reject Christ?

{Call on someone to answer.}

Why is it helpful to know why people reject Christ?

{Ask for a volunteer to answer. The answer is that knowing the real reason will help us to know how seriously to take their intellectual objections, and it may also give us the opportunity to help the non-Christian deal with the real issue.}

Is it ever helpful to respond to the "intellectual excuses" of a proud or rebellious person?

{Call on someone to answer. The answer is yes.}

Again, what is apologetics?

{Call on someone.}

Why should we study apologetics?

{Call on someone.}

Where is apologetics commanded in the Bible?

{Call on someone.}

When should we use apologetics, before or after the gospel?

{Call on someone.}

Who needs apologetics?

{Call on someone. The answer is: all Christians, and non-Christians who need to overcome intellectual obstacles to faith.}

Has anyone noticed what all five questions in the outline begin with? Right, a "w." Let's all say the "w" questions together beginning with "What is apologetics?"

{Recite the questions a couple times with the students.}

Now, to make sure you have become experts on this material, let's try something else. Turn to a partner and go through the lesson together, one of you asking the "W" questions and the other presenting the correct answers learned in class, without looking at your papers. After 2 minutes, switch roles. If you finish before the other pairs, evaluate each other's presentation according to the correct answers in your notes.

THE LAWS OF THE LEARNER APPLIED:

The Law of Retention is utilized here to get the students to remember this material. Through repetition, the material is reinforced in the students' minds.

VI. APPLICATION OF LESSON

A. This week, approach someone who is not a Christian and ask him for reasons for his unbelief. Try to discern why he is not a Christian. If he has intellectual problems with Christianity, find out what they are.

    You may want to lead your conversation to the subject by asking, "Do you consider yourself a Christian? Do you mind telling me why you choose not to be a Christian?"

B. Ask the same person if he believes truth is relative.

C. Share the "W" questions and answers with a friend or family member.

THE LAWS OF THE LEARNER APPLIED:

The application is the *Master* step of the Retention Method.

The second activity in the Application is to ask someone if he believes that truth is relative or if there are some things that are universally and objectively true. This question is related to the content of next week's lesson.

Next time we will discuss your interviews and then talk about four of the most common misconceptions that non-Christians have concerning Christianity!

NOTES

[1] *Why I Believe*, 13.

[2] The "secret volunteers" activity is found in a video curriculum, *Don't Leave Your Brains at the Door*, by Josh McDowell.

[3] The word *apologia* is also found in Acts 22:1.

[4] A logical account (the Greek word for reason is *logos*).

$\mathscr{2}$ COMMON MISCONCEPTIONS

THE LAWS OF THE LEARNER APPLIED:

The follow-up on the homework is the Improve and Inspire steps of the Equipping Method. The first words in bold are need-building comments that show the seriousness of the following objections.

{Draw the man on the path to the Cross with four obstructing rocks. Leave the diagram on the board during the lesson. After you refute each of the following misconceptions, have a student come up and erase one rock.}

Today, I'm going to present to you four of the most common misconceptions that non-Christians have concerning Christianity. In fact, many Christians tend to agree with the four erroneous statements that we will discuss. But these might obstruct a non-Christian on his way to the Cross. We need to remove these stones if they are in the way of someone becoming a Christian.

{Especially if you have a younger class, begin with a scientific experiment. Prove that the law of gravity exists by repeatedly dropping raw eggs into a cake pan on a large plastic sheet from gradually increased heights. Use a yardstick to measure the distance the eggs are dropped. (Have a damp rag near to wipe up any overspray later.) Have someone record the observations. For example: "The egg was dropped from a distance of 4 feet and splattered on the floor." This controlled repeatable experiment will prove gravity.}

THE LAWS OF THE LEARNER APPLIED:

This experiment will build the need and will help the student remember that Christianity cannot be proven with the "scientific method."

Misconception 1: "Christianity must be proven scientifically; I'll accept Christianity when you prove it with the scientific method."

{Try writing the capitalized words and talking at the same time.}

Can we prove Christianity is true the same way that we prove gravity exists? Why not? Because we prove gravity by the SCIENTIFIC METHOD, by having a CONTROLLED ENVIRONMENT where an EXPERIMENT is repeated again and again and observations recorded. The experiment must be REPEATABLE. The central claims of Christianity, which are the death, burial, and Resurrection {Sketch a diagram of the cross, the tomb, and the Resurrection.} of Jesus, are historical claims and cannot be repeated. You can't take Jesus, kill and bury him, and see if he resurrects again and again and again. Historical events are unrepeatable. You can't prove historical events using the scientific method. You must evaluate historical claims using the LEGAL-HISTORICAL METHOD of proof. How would you determine whether something occurred in history? Look at the WRITTEN testimony, the ORAL testimony, and the PHYSICAL testimony. How would a jury determine whether someone was guilty of a crime? Look at the written testimony against him, the oral testimony of those who watched it and were willing to testify, and look at the physical evidence, such as fingerprints. In the same way, Christianity, being historical, can be shown to be true using the legal-historical method.

The fact that Christianity's central claims (the death, burial, and Resurrection of Jesus) can be analyzed by the legal-historical method of proof makes it different from other religions. Unlike Christianity, many other religions

Scientific Method

- Controlled environment
- Experiment
- Repeatable

Legal Historical Method

- Written
- Oral
- Physical

cannot be proven true or false using the historical method. But *if* Christianity is true, it can be *proven* to be true, not by the scientific method, but by the legal-historical method.

This does not mean that science or the "sciences" such as archaeology or textual criticism[1] cannot be used to help confirm Christianity. In fact, scientific facts do a lot to support the validity of Christianity. I am simply saying you can't use what is called "the scientific method" to prove Christianity. You must use the legal-historical method of proof.

So, is it true that Christianity has to be proven with the scientific method?

{Wait for answer.}

No. How is it proven?

{Wait for answer.}

Once we show to a non-Christian that Christianity can be proven to be true with the legal-historical method, rather than the scientific method, we can move our non-Christian a little closer to the cross.

{Have a student erase one stone on the path to the Cross. As you go through these misconceptions and erase the stones, play this diagram up pretty big. Have fun with it. Act like you are eager to get the stick figure saved. That person is getting closer, and by the end of the session the class should be able to present the gospel to him. Then (since there will be no more objections) he may become a Christian.}

THE LAWS OF THE LEARNER APPLIED:

Having the student erase one stone will get them involved, helping them remember the misconception and feel the need to tackle it. The students will "feel" for the man stick figure on the board. The need will be built for removing those obstacles in his way.

Misconception 2: "I can't accept Christianity, because there isn't enough evidence for me to be 100% sure that it is true."

How would you respond to this?

{Wait for response.}

Is it possible to prove anything historical with 100% certainty?

{Wait for response; the answer is no.}

You [can't] prove anything historical with [100%] certainty.

For example: Julius Caesar crossing the Rubicon; George Washington being the first president of the U.S.; Abraham Lincoln being shot in Ford's Theatre.

In fact, we can't present 100% proof in any case in which we arrive at a conclusion inductively—by gathering evidence or data.

But do we have to have absolute evidence to make decisions? We make decisions every day based on the weight of the evidence—the probability that something happened or that something will happen. We would never get into a **car** {Draw a picture of a car on the board.} **to drive** someplace if we had to have absolute proof that we would get there safely. Juries would never convict someone if the prosecution had to produce 100% proof; they need only prove something beyond a reasonable doubt.

As apologists, we don't have to make an absolute case for Christianity; we need only show that the probability of Christianity being true is very high. And as Pascal (that famous French philosopher and physicist) said,

"There is [enough] evidence to convince anyone who is not set against it, but not enough to bring anyone into the kingdom who [will not come]" (Blaise Pascal).

The historical evidence for Christianity is not absolute, but it is sufficient.

{Have students get this last statement ("The historical evidence …") into their notes.}

In case you're wondering if this means that you can't know with certainty that you belong to the right religion, the answer is "You *can* know for sure that you are right." There is a difference between *PROVING* something absolutely and *KNOWING* something absolutely. You can know that Christianity is true with supreme certainty once you make a decision to follow Christ. When you stand on the foundation of the evidence, and take the step of faith {Take a literal step to illustrate.} necessary to embrace Christianity, the Holy Spirit will confirm in your heart that what you are believing is absolutely true. So you can *know* with certainty that it is true beyond the certainty with which you can *prove* it. You can come to the point where you can live as though you had 100% proof for the validity of Christianity. This is called *moral certainty*.

{Have someone come up and erase another rock from the skeptic's path.}

{Do the "Disappearing Penny Trick" (Supplemental Material section) and then show the optical illusion with the curved cards (May be ordered from Living Waters Publications, P.O. Box 1172, Bellflower, CA 90706, 1-800-437-1893; or from www.livingwaters.com).}

What I just showed you makes the point that what *appears* to be true isn't always what really *is* true. The penny was really under the glass whether you believed it was or not, *and* the cards were the same size whether you believed them to be or not. This helps answer the following misconception:

THE LAWS OF THE LEARNER APPLIED:

The glass and penny trick and the card illusion help build the need for the 3rd misconception— that truth is relative and dependent upon belief.

Misconception 3: "Truth is [relative]. If you believe something, that is truth for you."

Can anyone refute this misconception?

{Wait for response.}

The two illustrations I gave showed that something can be believed, and then shown later that it was false all along. Something can be absolutely true, while someone believes it to be false. Truth is not dependent on belief.

Suppose this were a science class, and there was a beaker of hydrochloric acid sitting on the desk.

THE LAWS OF THE LEARNER APPLIED:

The hydrochloric acid illustration will build the need and cause the student to remember. The story of the man on the construction crew will build the need for believing the right thing about reality. The sentence in a box is a need-builder. It attracts attention.

{Have a little beaker with a little water in it on your desk.}

Suppose one of you came in very thirsty and took a drink of it, {Pick the beaker up, and bring it to your lips.} **believing that it was Sprite. Even if you drank it fully believing that it was Sprite, what would happen?**

{Wait for response.}

Obviously, if someone drank the hydrocloric acid, he would be hurt very badly, even if he believed that the acid was Sprite. BELIEVING SOMETHING DOES NOT MAKE IT TRUE. If something is true, it is true whether we believe it or not. I know of someone on a construction crew who drank wood alcohol out of a milk jug container thinking that it was water. It killed him. {Pause.} **Is it true that believing something makes it true? No. We can demonstrate that very easily in the physical realm. And if someone says, "Well, it's different in the spiritual realm," he has no way of showing that to be the case. It makes sense that what is real is real regardless of our opinions about it, and what is true is true regardless of what we think.**

We are refuting the idea that truth is relative and dependent on belief for its truthfulness. This idea doesn't work in real life. The idea that truth is relative is also SELF-CONTRADICTORY. Someone who says this is actually saying that all truths are relative except for the truth that all things are relative. They are saying that there is only one absolute—the fact that there are no absolutes. This cannot be true because nothing is true that is self-contradictory. Here is another example of something that is self-refuting:

{Draw a box on the board with the sentence inside: "The sentence in this box is false." Explain how the sentence is true if it is false, and false if it is true. It is self-contradictory, self-refuting.}

The sentence in this box is false.

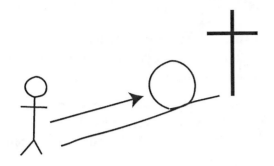

Misconception 4: "It doesn't matter what you believe as long as you are sincere in your faith. It really doesn't matter who or what you put your faith in. The important thing is that you believe—period."

THE LAWS OF THE LEARNER APPLIED:

The question and pause for disagreement will build the need for the answer especially since this statement goes against a common assumption that the students may have.

In the same way, the statement that there are no absolutes is a self-contradiction because the statement "There are no absolutes" is presented as an absolute.

{Have someone come up and erase another rock. Bring the stick figure man closer to the Cross.}

This last objection is related to the previous one:

How would you counter this misconception?

{Wait 4–5 seconds for response.}

This cannot be true. The object of our faith (what we put our faith in) is important. There is only one person who can save us—Jesus Christ. We must put our faith in Him. It will do us no good to put our faith in someone or something that cannot save us, no matter how sincere we are.

Did you know we are not saved by faith?

{Pause for reaction, possible disagreement by students.}

We are not saved by our faith; we are saved by *Christ* when we place our faith in Him. We are saved *by* grace (the grace of Christ) *through* faith. {Ephesians 2:8–9} If faith could save me, I could exercise faith in this light, {Point to light above you as you speak.} and I would be saved. This is not how it works. Again, only Christ can bring salvation.

{Bring two volunteers up; to make your point, label one a Muslim with strong faith, the other one a Christian with weak faith.}

Who is saved: this Muslim who has a strong faith in Mohammad's teaching or this Christian who has a weak (though real) faith in Christ?

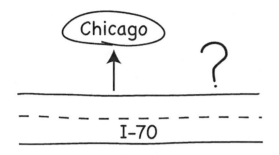

{Let the students answer.}

The Christian is the only one saved though he has a weaker faith. Why? Because he has his faith in the right person.

A lot of people say that any person in any religion will be saved as long as they are sincerely following the path that they were led onto. As long as they believe the road they are on is right, they will be O.K. But if I traveled Interstate 70, believing with all of my heart that it would take me to Chicago, would I get to Chicago?

{Illustrate this on the marker board. You may want to use another road that the students are familiar with and another familiar town that the road doesn't go to.}

{Wait for response.}

No, I wouldn't, no matter how sincere I was in my faith. The Bible says that there is a way that seems right unto a man, but the end thereof is death (Proverbs 14:12).

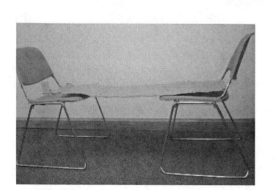

{Place a strip of cardboard between two chairs. Have someone walk across the cardboard. He will fall between the chairs. Have him get up. Tell him he needs to have more faith. Have the rest of the class chant, "Faith, Faith... ." Of course he will fall again. Then put a sturdy board between the chairs. Have the student cross. He will do so successfully. Have the students answer the question: "Does it matter what the object of your faith is?"}

{Have the students pair up. One student is the "skeptic"; the other is the "apologist." The "skeptic" will bring up the last two misconceptions; the "apologist" refutes them, using the material just presented. Give them about 3 minutes. Listen in to see if they "got the hang of it." If you (the teacher) feel prepared, offer to field any questions that may have come out of the little debates.}

{Have a student come up and erase the last rock blocking the path that leads to the Cross. Have a student (who knows how to share the gospel) get the stick figure "saved."}

APPLICATION OF LESSON:

This week, find someone who believes at least one of the four misconceptions we talked about today. To determine whether someone has these misconceptions, ask questions such as: "How would Christianity have to be proven if it could be proven?" "How much proof would you need to believe in Christianity?" "Is truth relative?" and "How important is it that you believe in the right thing or person?"

For any of the misconceptions, go on the offensive. Ask the skeptic why he is so sure that he is believing the right thing about the issue. Ask him for his reasons. If he says, "You can't prove what you believe," say, "Then prove to me what you believe." If he says that all religions are true, ask, "What happens if you're wrong, and all religions don't lead to God?" After you have put him on the defensive, share with him the illustrations and arguments from the notes. Do not be argumentative!

Take notes of your dialogue to share in class.

THE LAWS OF THE LEARNER APPLIED:

The Application is the *Master* step of the Retention Method. It will also give the teacher an opportunity to *Improve* and *Inspire* the students.

We will talk about your discussions with your skeptic friend at the beginning of our next class.

Today we talked about 4 common misconceptions of the basic nature of Christianity. Next week we will begin to discuss other objections that can also serve as intellectual obstacles to faith. When you come for the rest of the lessons in this course, you will learn what these objections are and how to respond to them!

NOTES

[1] Textual criticism is the science that compares existing manuscripts to determine the original text of ancient books. You'll discuss this science in Lesson Seven.

3 IS THERE A GOD?

{Give Quiz #1 (p. 155 in the Supplemental section). See how much students remember from the first two lessons. Limit the time of the quiz and quickly move through the answers when most are finished. Total time: 7 minutes. After the quiz, have the students turn to Lesson 3 in their notes.}

{Follow up on last week's assignment. Have a discussion for 3–4 minutes. Motivate students to continue to talk to unbelievers.}

I. CAN ANYONE KNOW THERE IS NOT A GOD?

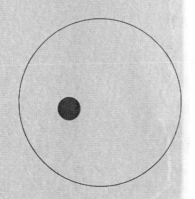

{Bring up one of the students and have him pretend that he is an atheist. Say the following to him.}

"So you're an atheist. That's interesting. Well, I have a question for you. Let's say that this big circle {Draw a circle on the board.} **represents all the knowledge of the universe. How much of the total knowledge of the universe do you think you possess? Here's the marker. Draw a circle within this circle to represent the knowledge that you have."**

{The "atheist" will then draw a circle or dot inside the larger circle. Then point to the area outside his circle.}

II. PASCAL'S WAGER

Either God exists or He doesn't exist. What would be wiser—to believe He does exist or to believe He doesn't exist? Let's say we put a wager on the idea that God exists. If we win this wager, and He does exist, we win everything; if we lose, and God doesn't exist, we lose [nothing]. Since this is the case, we should wager that God [does] exist.

"Is it possible that the knowledge of God exists in this area, but that you just don't know it yet?"

{Wait for response.}

"So it is possible that God does exist, right? Maybe you don't believe He exists, but since you can't *know* that He *doesn't* exist, then I would say that you are really an agnostic, someone who *doesn't know* God exists. If you say that you *cannot* know God exists (like 'hard agnostic'), maybe the knowledge that you can know exists outside your present knowledge."

{Allow for feedback from "atheist." He should reluctantly agree with your point. Continue talking to him through the next section as well. Have fun with this.}

"Since no one can prove that God doesn't exist, then maybe you ought to consider Pascal's Wager. Have you ever heard of Blaise Pascal? He was a famous French physicist and philosopher who had become a Christian. He challenged people with something like this:

"More importantly, if we wager that God *doesn't* exist, and He *does*, then we have lost everything.... Does this make sense to you?"

{The "atheist" should then say something like: "That would make sense if there were any evidence at all for the existence of God. But I am willing to take my chances, because I don't think you have any convincing evidence at all."}

"But there is a lot of evidence for the existence of God. I want to show some of that to you now. After I have shared this with you, I would like you to reconsider Pascal's Wager. I think you will have seen enough evidence for God to believe that it is too risky to *not* believe in Him. Even if there were only a 20% chance that God exists, that would still be too risky. I'm pretty sure that you would not get on a plane if you knew there was a 20% chance that it would go down."

{Send the "atheist" back to his seat after thanking him for his help.}

III. EVIDENCE FOR THE EXISTENCE OF GOD

Let's look at some of the arguments for the existence of God. First, there is the **COSMOLOGICAL ARGUMENT.**

A. The Cosmological Argument

The Cosmological Argument begins with the idea that everything must have an adequate explanation. For example, let's say that you came in here today and saw a big gorilla sitting on the front row, eating a bowl of corn flakes. You would not just think that it popped out of nothing. You would wonder where it came from and how it got here. You would need an explanation. Everything must have an adequate explanation, including the universe as a whole.

The word *cosmological* comes from *cosmos*, which means "world." The cosmological argument demands an adequate explanation for the existence of the world, or universe.

The argument says that:

1. The universe could not have come from nothing.

2. The universe could not have always existed as it is.

3. The universe could not have come from impersonal matter or energy.

Therefore, it must have been created by a personal, eternal, self-existent Being. This is the only explanation that makes sense, since the other options are not valid.

Let's discuss further the possible explanations for the universe. I will show you why the non-theistic explanations are not valid.

The universe could not have come from nothing.

Why do we state that it is unreasonable to say that the universe came from nothing?

{Get responses from students. They should be able to see how ridiculous this idea is.}

Well, think about it. How could nothing produce something? Nothing would have to be something already in order to produce something else. So then nothing would not really be nothing, but something, if it were going to create the universe. If we say that the universe created itself, we would have to say that it existed before it existed, in order to create its own existence. Something would have to be and not be at the same time and in the same respect. This is self-contradictory, and ridiculous.

The universe could not have always existed as it is.

What is the problem with the idea that the universe has always existed?

{Get responses from students. If they give good answers, commend them.}

The two LAWS OF THERMODYNAMICS are very problematic to the idea that the universe has always existed as it is. The first law states that matter/energy can neither be created nor destroyed. The second law states that the usable energy in the universe is being converted slowly into unusable energy. When you put the two laws together, you have a fixed amount of energy in the universe, but an energy that is depleting (in terms of usability). What is the significance of this? The universe is slowly dying. If it has always existed as it does now (including the natural laws of the universe), the energy in the world would already be all used up, everything would be at the same temperature (heat death), and we would all be dead.

The universe could not have come from impersonal matter/energy.

Why is it unreasonable to say that the universe came from impersonal matter or energy?

{Get responses from students.}

If you could get around the laws of thermodynamics (which you can't, even in this scenario), then you would still have a very serious problem. If the universe came from an impersonal "speck" or "blob" {Draw a "blob" (a very wobbly circle) on the board, then next to it write: + time + chance.}, **then the only factors that exist are the impersonal, plus time, plus chance.**

Francis Schaeffer said:

+ TIME + CHANCE

"Beginning with the impersonal, everything, including man, must be explained in terms of the impersonal plus time plus [chance]. Do not let anyone divert your mind at this point. There are no other factors in the formula, because there are no other factors that exist... . No one has ever demonstrated how time plus chance, beginning with an impersonal, can produce the needed complexity of the universe, let alone the [personality] of man."[1]

Therefore, the universe must have been created by a personal, eternal Being.

The only reasonable explanation for the universe is a self-existent Creator.

This is the Cosmological Argument for God's existence.

One aspect of the Cosmological Argument is so significant that it has its own name—the "Teleological Argument." The word *teleological* comes from *telos*, which means "end, or goal." It has to do with purpose, or design.

B. The Teleological Argument

The TELEOLOGICAL ARGUMENT says that:

All the intricate design in the universe argues for a [purposeful] first cause.

For example,

* The Eye

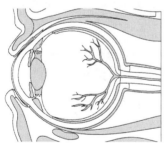

{Show a diagram of the eye (larger picture in the Supplement section). Point out some of the complexity; discuss our amazing ability to see. Some say the eye is actually a poor design. To refute this idea, see www.answersingenesis.org/go/eye.}

* The Cell

{Show a diagram of the cell, supplemental section}.

Look at the cell, the parts of which all need to be functioning simultaneously for the cell to survive. If evolution occurred, these cell parts must have appeared spontaneously, all at the same time. But this sounds too much like creation. It would have been impossible for a structure with this much design and purpose to have come into being by chance.

- DNA

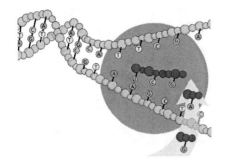

Look at the structure of a single strand of DNA. {Show diagram of DNA, Supplemental section.} **It is more complex than a modern computer. All the information of the human body is stored in a strand of human DNA that takes up less space than the period at the end of a written sentence.** {Make a tiny dot on the board with your marker as you say this.} **The amount of information that could be stored in a pinhead's volume of DNA is equivalent to a pile of paperback books 500 times as high as the distance from earth to the moon, each with a different, yet specific content.[2] DNA's order and complexity show that it must have been designed by a great Intelligence.**

{Review the Cosmological and Teleological Arguments.}

THE LAWS OF THE LEARNER APPLIED:

Reviewing the material will help the student "master the minimum."

Let's review a little bit. What are the two arguments for the existence of God we just talked about?

{Wait for someone to answer.}

What does the Cosmological Argument say?

{Call on someone you think could answer correctly.}

Why couldn't the universe come from nothing?

{Wait for someone to answer.}

Why couldn't the universe come from an impersonal "blob"?

{Ask for a response from someone who hasn't answered yet.}

What does the Teleological Argument say?

{Ask for a response from someone who hasn't answered yet.}

What are three examples of the complexity of life, and thus the necessity of Intelligent Design?

{Call on a quieter student.}

What information can fit into a strand of DNA, which is no bigger that a dot on piece of paper?

{Wait for someone to answer.}

C. The Anthropic Principle

Our third argument for the existence of God is The ANTHROPIC PRINCIPLE. This says that:

The earth has just the right conditions for human life.

For example,

- Distance from the sun

{Draw a sun and a stick figure representing all of us.}

If we were any closer to the sun, we would burn up. If we were any farther away, we would freeze to death. The earth's atmosphere is just right to support life. People take for granted all the things that we experience that are necessary for life to exist on this planet. The only adequate explanation for this is that the earth and its atmosphere were made for us by an intelligent Being.

- Gravity and electromagnetism

All the unrelated constants in physics are precisely the values necessary for a world to produce life. These next two points are examples of this. Patrick Glynn writes in *God: The Evidence*.

"Gravity is roughly 10^{39} times weaker than electromagnetism. If gravity had been [10^{33}] times weaker than electromagnetism, stars would be a billion times less massive and would burn a [million] times faster."

{Make sure you write "10^{33}" on the board}

Also,

• Protons and neutrons

"If the difference in mass between a proton and a neutron were not exactly as it is—roughly [twice] the mass of an electron—then all neutrons would have become protons or vice versa."

"Say good-bye to chemistry as we know it—and to life."

Glynn also says, "The very nature of water—so vital to life—is something of a mystery... . Unique amongst the molecules, water is lighter in its solid than liquid form:

{Illustrate this with a glass of ice water.}

• The nature of water

"Ice floats. If it did not, the oceans would freeze from the bottom up, and earth would now be covered with [solid ice]."

The MORAL ARGUMENT says that:

D. The Moral Argument

The fact that we all have a sense of right and wrong argues that there is a Supreme [Lawgiver] from which that morality comes.

C.S. Lewis is famous for his presentation of this argument in his *Mere Christianity*. Lewis talked about a sense of "oughtness" that people from every culture have. Different cultures sometimes disagree about what is right and what is wrong, but all persons experience times when they know that they "ought" to do something, or "ought not" do something else. Where did this sense of "oughtness" come from, if not from God?

{Ask the class "atheist" what arguments for God he or she found most compelling. Ask him to give reasons for his choices. Ask him if he would, in light of this evidence, be willing to risk losing his soul in Hell by choosing not to believe in God. Introduce the next section by having him bring up the following objection (prepare him before class).}

IV. Responding to the #1 Objection to the Existence of God:

"If there is a good and omnipotent God, then why is there evil and suffering in the world? The existence of evil must prove there is not a good, omnipotent God."

That is the #1 objection to the existence of God. Do you see why people would think this? People expect a good, all-powerful God to immediately deal with sin and suffering. They say that if this God were real, He would keep the world free of pain. If He were good, He would not want there to be sin or suffering. If He were all-powerful, He could do something about it. So WHY then is there EVIL in the world?

How do we respond to this question?

{Take some time to see how the students are able to answer this question.}

Answers:

• The problem of evil implies that there is a God.

What is so interesting about this problem of evil is that the very problem implies that there is a God. For we would not know that evil exists without an absolute standard of right and wrong by which we could distinguish good from bad. This absolute standard of right and wrong must come from an Absolute Lawgiver, who is God. This goes back to what we were

saying about the moral argument for the existence of God.

But why *is* there evil in the world?

{Have students try to answer before you continue.}

- There is evil in the world because the first humans God made abused their [freedom] and chose to disobey God. Suffering is the consequence of [moral] evil.

The first two humans, Adam and Eve, disobeyed God, and as a result, the whole world was cursed (Gen. 3:14–19; Rom. 8:20–23). Even innocent people suffer because of this curse on the whole world.

But why did God make free creatures?

{Have students try to answer before you continue.}

- God made free creatures because He wanted them to [love] Him.

Love is impossible without freedom of choice. God couldn't make men and women love Him. Forced love is a contradiction.

Someone may say, "I understand now why there is suffering in the world. It is the consequence of moral evil. But why does there have to be as much suffering in the world as there is?"

How would you respond to this question?

{Have students try to answer before you continue.}

No doubt there would be more suffering in the world if it wasn't for God's mercy. But because the world needs to be taught how serious sin is, God doesn't eliminate all suffering.

- The great amount of suffering in the world shows how [serious] sin is.

It is so serious that drastic consequences have come into the world as a result of sin.

But some may say, "Why doesn't God do something about all the evil and suffering in the world?"

How would you answer this question?

{Get a response or two from the class.}

The answer is that God has *already* done something about it. God the Son entered our pain and suffering with us, so that we could be freed from sin, and someday escape our suffering forever.

When we personally experience pain here and now, we are not without consolation. If we are true Christians, we can have the assurance that "all things work together for good to them that love God"—that's what the Bible says (Romans 8:28). Though we may not understand it, God has a purpose for what He allows in our lives. God takes the pain we experience and causes it to work for our best interest.

God uses suffering many times to draw people into a relationship with Himself. C.S. Lewis said, "God whispers to us in our pleasure, speaks in our conscience, but shouts in our pain. It is God's megaphone to rouse a deaf world."[3]

{Before class is over, direct students to the following application. Encourage them to share this information with a non-believer (even an atheist) this coming week.}

APPLICATION

This week, show someone (preferably an atheist) the circle illustration, Pascal's Wager, and at least 3 arguments for the existence of God.

NOTES

[1] Francis Schaeffer, *He is There and He is Not Silent*, Tyndale House, Carol Stream, Illinois, pp. 7–8, 1980.
[2] W. Gitt, Dazzling design in miniature, *Creation* **20**(1):6, 1997.
[2] C.S. Lewis, *The Problem of Pain*, Macmillan Publishing, New York, p. 93, 1962.

4 CREATION APOLOGETICS

{Materials: deck of UNO cards, marker, marker board, several coins, dice, pail, 10 CDs numbered 1–10, box of rags. You may want to make your own (big) dice out of thick paper. Templates to use for this are available on the Internet—search for "paper dice."}

{Follow up on last week's assignment.}

{Pull out box of rags and put it in a corner where all can see. Then say the next two sentences with a twinkle in your eye.}

I want you to keep one eye on that box of rags over there. Something may come out of it.

In the meantime, let's start our lesson.

In this lesson, we'll dig a little deeper into the evidence that we were created by God. One of the most amazing things about humans is how hard some of us will try to explain our existence apart from a Creator. All kinds of books have been written by those who want to refute the teaching that we were made by God. These people claim that creation is not true science; they'll argue that real science cannot allow the supernatural to be an explanation for anything. To them, everything has to be explained by natural causes. But there is something that is true about *both* the claim that everything has evolved through "natural" processes *and* the

---

THE LAWS OF THE LEARNER APPLIED:

Starting off by referring to the box of rags may help to build the need. It may get the attention of the students and make them curious. Asking students what is true about evolution and creation will get them to think. Writing on the board will keep students' attention and help retention.

claim that we have been created by God. What is that? What is true about both the claim for evolution and the claim for creation?

{Wait for response. Write "Creation vs. Evolution" on the board.}

*Both the claim for EVOLUTION and the claim for CREATION are propositions that have to be [taken by faith].

Evolution and creation are BOTH FAITH PROPOSITIONS.

Neither is strictly scientific since both creation and evolution are trying to explain what happened in the past. This is really an *historical* issue. None of us saw how the world was formed. We observed neither the creation nor the evolution of the horse, for instance. Since none of us were around to see either evolution or creation occur, we'll either have to take someone else's word for it or look for clues in the world around us.

If we really were created by God, don't you think it makes sense that He would find some way to communicate to us the truth about our origin and our purpose for being here?

{Get response from students.}

It makes sense that if there is a God who made us, He would let us know about that. As you know, there is a Book that claims to be written by God. In this Book, God claims to have made the world and everything in it in 6 days. Sharing our faith would be much easier if people would simply accept this Book's word for it, wouldn't it?

{For younger class, ask if they know what the name of this book is; get response.}

In a future lesson, I plan to start talking about the evidence that the Bible really was written by God. If we can persuade people that the

Bible is from God, then we can encourage them to trust what God said in his Word about origins.

While we are trying to convince non-Christians of the truth of the Bible, we also need to point them to the world around us and help them see that the biblical account of origins makes the most sense of the world. So to an extent we can use science to make our case for a Creator. We can't use the scientific method *itself* to determine the historical event of creation (you can't put the beginning of the universe into a test tube), but we can show people how the scientific evidence supports the biblical view of creation. It would be like looking at the fingerprint evidence at a crime scene to help determine which person committed the murder. We can look at scientific evidence like DNA to show that *God* committed the act of Creation, not time and chance.

One way to approach this is to look at what evolutionists or creationists would expect to see if their belief were true. If evolution were true, what would we expect to see?

{Wait for response. Try to get at least three students to make comments. Correct answers would include: lots of transitional forms in the fossil record, evidence of mutations producing new information, simplicity rather than complexity, randomness in how the world operates, etc.}

If creation were true, what would we expect to see?

{Wait for response. Try to get at least three students to make comments. Correct answers would include: evidence of design (intricate complexity), limits to variations within kinds of plants and animals, evidence of distinct kinds in the fossil record, established laws of science that show that the universe was put in place by an unchanging Master Designer, etc.}

THE LAWS OF THE LEARNER APPLIED:

Asking these questions will help build the need for the forthcoming information and will also help them understand the point of the lesson better.

Does what we see around us best fit the expectations of *evolution* or *creation*?

Which approach is most consistent with the [evidence]?

Once we know what each would predict, then we can observe the world and ask:

Or put another way:

Since scientists have special tools for study, they can make even deeper observations than we can. What have they discovered? Do the results of their observations better fit with evolution or creation?

What I want us to do today is give you more of the evidence that shows that the world around us fits the expectations (or predictions) of creation, not evolution. I want you to be able to share with your friends how the established laws of science and other data support the biblical record of creation more than naturalistic evolution. In fact, I'll show you that evolution really is anti-scientific.

I want us to first look at one of the most basic laws of science, the Law of Biogenesis.

I. THE LAW OF BIOGENESIS

A hundred years ago or so, people used to believe that life could spontaneously generate. They thought that, for instance, if you left a box of rags in the corner long enough, it might spontaneously generate mice—from the non-living rags.

{Point to the box of rags in the corner.}

Do you think that this box of rags we've been waiting on could ever spontaneously generate mice?

{Get response from students.}

No? Well, you are enlightened. ☺ In times past, some people thought that it could. But the famous scientist LOUIS PASTEUR (a Christian, by the way) and others did many experiments that disproved the idea that life could come from non-life. They recognized the LAW OF BIOGENESIS. Can anyone tell me what the Law of Biogenesis is?

{Wait for response.}

The Law of Biogenesis: [Life] only comes from [life].

But evolutionists deny this basic law of science when they say that life had to come from non-life at least once. Though they see it as problematic, most of them still think that life spontaneously arose out of some "primordial soup." The evolutionist George Wald stated in the *Scientific American*:

"One has only to contemplate the magnitude of this task to concede that the spontaneous generation of a living organism is impossible. Yet here we are—as a result, I believe, of spontaneous generation" (Harvard University biochemist and Nobel Laureate George Wald, 1954 in *Scientific American*).

Why do you think people like George Wald continue to believe in (or at least teach) spontaneous generation, even when they know it is scientifically impossible?

{Wait for response. Answers might include peer pressure, not wanting to be accountable to God, no other naturalistic explanation, etc.}

Actually, some atheistic evolutionists have accepted the fact that life could not and did not arise spontaneously on this planet. They come up with non-theistic solutions. For instance,

A few evolutionists propose that life was transported from another [planet] to the earth.

Francis CRICK, famous as the co-discoverer of the structure of DNA, believed in this theory, called *panspermia*. But what is the problem with Crick's theory?

{Wait for response. Answer: It doesn't solve the problem of spontaneous generation; it simply moves the problem to a different part of the universe!}

What does this ultimately mean?

Evolution is not [scientific] when it comes to the Law of Biogenesis vs. Spontaneous Generation.

Evolutionists contradict one of the most basic laws of science!

Let's take a minute to review what we have just discussed:

{Get a response for each of these questions:}

1. What is one thing that creationists and evolutionists have in common?

2. In this lesson we are talking about whether creation or evolution is more consistent with what?

3. What is the Law of Biogenesis?

4. What theory does the Law of Biogenesis disprove?

5. Since it is scientifically impossible for life to come from non-life, what is one solution that some atheistic scientists have proposed?

6. What is the problem with the idea that life was transported from another planet?

THE LAWS OF THE LEARNER APPLIED:

Reviewing will help the student remember the material. Taking notes will also help retention.

II. THE LAWS OF PROBABILITY

I want to spend most of our time today talking about the probability of life occurring by chance.

Most evolutionists say that given enough time even spontaneous generation can occur. This is what the evolutionist George Wald said:

"Time is in fact the hero of the plot. The time with which we have to deal is of the order of two billion years. What we regard as impossible on the basis of human experience is meaningless there. Given so much time, the 'impossible' becomes possible; the possible probable, and the probable virtually certain. One has only to wait; time itself performs the miracles" (Harvard University biochemist and Nobel Laureate George Wald, 1954 in *Scientific American*).

Do you see how the evolutionist views time as almost God? It is time that works miracles. For an evolutionist, turning a frog into a prince is a fairy tale unless you add a few hundred million years; then, a frog turning into a prince is science. Time (with chance) is the key. But Christians believe that time was part of creation. Evolutionists are taking part of creation and making it God. We know, though, that time and chance do not have the ability to create all the complexities of the universe.

{Review quote by Francis Schaeffer in previous lesson.}

{Pull out a deck of UNO® cards.}

This deck of UNO® cards is partially organized, since it wasn't shuffled since we last played the game, but let's take some time here to shuffle it.

{Shuffle the cards as you talk.}

As an evolutionist, I think that if I take enough time shuffling, I will actually be able to get all the cards in order.

{Pause as you shuffle the cards a bit.}

Now am I really going to be able to get the cards in order?

{Wait for response.}

Why do we shuffle cards? To make them more random, not less. Since we want the game to be fair, we mix up the cards as much as possible. The longer I shuffle, the more random it gets. The cards will not get more orderly by my spending more time shuffling. It is ludicrous to think that time can create order.

The laws of probability can help us understand how ridiculous it is to think that time and chance created life.

{Illustrate the following presentation with coins, dice, and ten disks, numbered 1–10. You will show the students that the laws of probability are definitely not on the side of evolution.}

{The next part of the lesson is an adaptation of an article called "Evolution, Chance and Creation" by Michael Stubbs, published on the Answers in Genesis website (www.answersingenesis.org/creation/v4/i2/chance.asp).}

Here's a question for you:

Is there enough time in the universe for [CHANGE] to produce the intricate [design] we see around us?

A few moments of easy mathematics will help us answer that question.

When we toss a coin, we expect it to land showing either a head or a tail.

{Toss a coin.}

We say from experience that the probability of the coin landing "heads" is one half, or we can say "tails" has a 50% chance of showing up. We also know from experience that this does not mean when we throw a head first, the next throw will be a tail. It simply means that if we keep tossing coins long enough, then on average half the time the coin lands, it will show heads, and half the time tails.

An interesting situation arises when two separate events occur at the same time; for example, tossing a coin and throwing a die. (Maybe you would call it a dice, but that is plural for more than one die.) If we ask:

What is the "chance" of getting a [head] and throwing a six at the same time?

A simple look at all the possible results of tossing coins and throwing dice will show the answer.

Since the coin has two sides and only one head, the possibility of a head is 1/2.

{Write: "chance of head: 1/2" on board.}

Since the die has six sides and only one face with six dots on it, the possibility of six is 1/6.

{Write "chance of 6 is 1/6" on board.}

{Toss the coin and die, 2–3 times, showing results.}

The only trouble is that:

Half of the time the die lands showing a six, the coin will show a tail, the other half of the times we throw a six, the coin would show a [head]. So the probability of throwing the head and the six together, must be one-half of the sixes, or put mathematically, 1/2 x 1/6. This, of course, is [1/12].

{Write on board "1/2 x 1/6 = 1/12".}

Statisticians have made this into a rule called the [MULTIPLICATON] RULE OF PROBABILITY.

This states that the chance of several independent results occurring at once is found by multiplying the mathematical probabilities of obtaining the individual results.

Let us extend this idea further. I have here a bucket in which are placed ten identical discs, each numbered from 1–10.

THE LAWS OF THE LEARNER APPLIED:

Using these hands-on illustrations will help students become more interested in the subject and will help them better understand and remember.

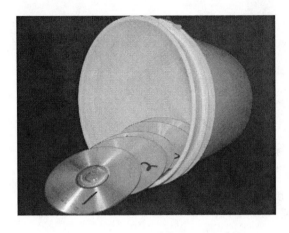

{Pull out bucket with pre-labeled disks—you could use CDs.}

The question is: Can chance methods enable us to count from 1 to 10? If only one disc is to be selected from the bucket, noted and replaced, and we require disc 1 first, disc 2 second in the correct sequence from 1–10, what is the probability of selecting all ten discs in order?

Let's actually start with an easier question: What is the probability of selecting disk 1 with one attempt?

{Wait for response.}

The math is relatively easy. Since there is only one disc numbered 1, there can be only one chance in ten (1/10) of selecting it. After we replace the first disc, the chance of selecting the disc number 2 is the same—1/10.

{For fun, see how long it takes someone to draw out the disk labeled "1." Use students who are not always volunteering.}

In fact, every separately numbered disc has one chance in ten of being selected. The probability of selecting the first one followed by the second one in correct order must be 1/10 x 1/10 or 1/100.

{Once the "1" is taken out, put it back in and see if someone can pick out the "2" (first try).}

To select all 10 disks in the right order the probability is 1/10 x 1/10 x 1/10 x 1/10 x 1/10 x 1/10 x 1/10 x 1/10 x 1/10 x 1/10 or $(1/10)^{10}$.

{Write out $(1/10^{10})$.}

This means that you would select the right order only once in 10 billion attempts.

{Write out "1 in 10 billion."}

"Chance" requires [10 billion] attempts, on the average, to count from 1 to 10.

What is the expected probability for chance to spell the phrase—"THE THEORY OF EVOLUTION"?

"Chance" will, on the average, spell "the theory of evolution" correctly only 1 in [(27^{23})] outcomes.

This computes to one success in 8.3 hundred quadrillion quadrillion attempts [(8.3×10^{32})]!

Put another way,

As you can see, chance isn't very efficient in producing design. To further illustrate that fact, I am now going to show you something fascinating. The question is:

This phrase by chance would involve the random selection and sequencing of letters and spaces in the correct order. Each letter from the alphabet plus one space (totaling 27 possible selections) has 1 chance in 27 of being selected. There are 20 letters plus 3 spaces in the phrase—"the theory of evolution."

{Write out: "26 letters in alphabet plus one space = 27; 20 letters + 3 spaces = 23.}

Therefore,

{Write out: "1 in $(27)^{23}$."}

{Write out "1 in (8.3×10^{32})."}

Suppose "chance" uses a machine which removes, records, and replaces all the letters randomly at the fantastic speed of one billion per microsecond (one quadrillion per second). On average the phrase would happen once in 25 billion years by this random method.

If, as evolutionists would have us believe, the earth has been in existence for approximately [5 billion] years, then "chance" could take [five] times this time to spell out "the theory of evolution," even at one billion attempts per microsecond, a phenomenal rate of experimentation.

And this phrase is infinitely simpler than the smallest lifeform, and children of average intelligence could spell "the theory of evolution" in less than a minute.

{End of adapted article.}

So you see it takes intelligence to produce life. Time and chance could not have produced life. The laws of probability disprove that.

The scientist/mathematician William Dembski explains that if something happening has a probability of less than 1 in 10^{150}, then it could not have occurred. The 10^{150} number is based on three things: the number of atoms in the universe (10^{80}), the number of seconds that have passed (according to evolutionists, 10^{25}), and the maximum number of changes a particle could go through (10^{45} alterations per second). {Write these numbers on the board.} **So,**

According to Dembski, if anything has had less than 1 in [10^{150}] chance of happening, it just could not have happened by chance.

This concept is part of Dembski's "Law of Small Probability."

But what do evolutionists say themselves about the probabilities of life evolving?

Evolutionist Julian Huxley said that the odds that the horse evolved was 1 chance in [$10^{3,000,000}$], but that it still happened thanks to natural selection, or the survival of the fittest.

However, natural selection is not a force with

any real intelligence; it could not therefore be a major factor at all. Compare $10^{3,000,000}$ to 10^{150}. According to Huxley's numbers there is no way evolution could occur.

Sir Fred Hoyle, the famous British mathematician and astronomer, said that the probability of life arising by chance was 1 in $10^{4,000}$, and that this is like rolling a "6" on a die 5,000,000 times in a row. Compare $10^{4,000}$ to 10^{150}. Life could not have arisen by chance.

{Write out the above numbers.}

Conclusion: Evolution is not consistent with the laws of probability.

Evolutionists are in denial when they refuse to face the impossible odds of evolution occurring and accept the implications of this impossibility.

So, based on what we have talked about so far, is evolution really scientific? Why not?

{Wait for response.}

Let's review a little more: To count from one to ten, "chance" would have to take, on the average, how many attempts?

{Call on someone.}

According to William Dembski, anything with less than 1 in _____ chance of happening could not have happened. (Fill in the blank.)

{Call on another student.}

What did Huxley say was the probability of a horse evolving?

{Call on another student.}

What did Fred Hoyle say was the probability of life arising by chance?

{Ask for volunteer to answer.}

So today we've talked about the Law of

Biogenesis and the Laws of Probability. We have seen that evolution does not follow these laws of science. The next time we meet we will talk about the laws of thermodynamics, the laws of genetics, the fossil record, and the age of the earth.

APPLICATION:

Make a list of people that you think need to hear these creation evidences. Pray for good opportunities to share this information with them.

5 MORE CREATION APOLOGETICS

{Follow up on last week's assignment. Ask students if they identified people that need to be presented with creation apologetics.}

I. THE LAWS OF THERMODYNAMICS

We talked about the Laws of Thermodynamics in lesson three, but let's review them. What is the First Law of Thermodynamics?

{Wait for response. The first law states that matter/energy can neither be created nor destroyed. (Obviously the existing matter had to come from somewhere; the law is not denying the original creation from an out-side Source—God, but it is denying that new matter/energy somehow appears out of nothing.)}

What is the Second Law of Thermodynamics?

{Wait for response. The second law states that the amount of usable energy in the universe is depleting. It is changing from usable energy to unusable energy, which is called "increasing entropy."}

These laws state that there is a fixed amount of matter/energy in the universe and that this fixed amount of energy is becoming more and more unusable. The universe is becoming more and more "run down." So how does this contradict evolution?

{Wait for response from students.}

Atheistic evolutionists have to say that matter/ energy came from nothing or that it has always existed. Obviously, the first option contradicts the First Law of Thermodynamics (matter can't come from nothing). The second option (that the universe has always existed) contradicts the Second Law of Thermodynamics. How does teaching the eternality of the universe contradict the Second Law of Thermodynamics?

{Wait for a student to answer.}

If the universe has always existed with a [fixed] amount of energy, and more and more of this energy has become [unusable], then by now the universe would be [completely] "run down" and we wouldn't be here!

Evolutionists are unscientific when they contradict the laws of thermodynamics.

II. THE FOSSIL RECORD

If evolution were true, then you would expect to see thousands of transitional forms in the fossil record. But after more than 150 years of digging, there are [fewer] examples of so-called transitional forms than in Darwin's day.

This lack of transitional forms is so obvious that now many evolutionists are admitting that there may not be any transitional forms. But instead adopting a belief in special creation, most of these evolutionists come up with other explanations. Some, like Stephen Gould, say that evolution happened in "spurts," relatively speaking. According to Gould, the fossil record comes from more stable and lengthy periods. The time during which the transitional forms lived was so short that we don't have fossils from that period.

Can someone tell me what is wrong with this explanation?

{Get someone to respond. Answer: These evolutionists are not arguing based on evidence, but they are instead making excuses for the lack of evidence. Actually, what they are discovering (lack of fossils of transitional forms) goes against the predictions of evolution: evolution would expect to find transitional forms in the fossil record.}

Creationists predict that there would be [distinct] "kinds" of organisms, based on what God made on Day 3, Day 5, and Day 6 of Creation Week. [Distinct] kinds of plants and animals are what we see in the fossil record.

|1|2|3|4|5|6|

{Review what God created on each of the six days of creation. This is important to do especially if the students are not very familiar with the Creation Week.}

The fossil record suggests that the biblical creation is a much more [reasonable] proposition than evolution.

III. THE LAWS OF GENETICS

Here are some different pictures of dogs.

{Show to the class several pictures of various kinds of dogs (see Supplement section).}

I have a question for you. How many dogs were taken into Noah's Ark?

{Get response. The answer is "2."}

Well, then why are there so many different kinds of dogs in the world?

{Get response. Then, if they don't come up with the right answer, say that you will explain it in a little bit.}

Evolutionists argue that the variations among the kinds of animals, such as all the different kinds of dogs, are [proof] of the evolution that occurred through [mutations] and natural selection.

But most of the changes we see within different kinds of animals are not due to mutations, but to different combinations of genetic information that has [always] been in their DNA.

THE LAWS OF THE LEARNER APPLIED:

Showing pictures will help fulfill the Laws of Need and Retention.

The various breeds of dogs that we see today actually have [less] genetic information than the original dog kind, not [more] information.

They say that genetic mutations (acted on by natural selection) make the changes in organisms that are necessary to produce new kinds of plants and animals.

Look at all the varieties of dogs, for example. Are the differences between the beagle and the dalmation the result of genetic mutations?

{Show them the pictures of dogs again (in Supplemental section). Wait for response.}

No. Mendel's Laws of Genetics explain how various combinations of recessive and dominant genes produce different features in offspring. A Cocker Spaniel is not different from a Collie because of mutations, but because a certain portion of the dog population was separated from the rest and interbred. The genes for being a Cocker Spaniel were already part of the larger dog gene pool. Though mutations are real and can have some effect on populations, the vast majority of the various characteristics we see in the different varieties of dogs are the result of the breaking out of the larger gene pool and interbreeding.

And interbreeding (and selective breeding) can only accomplish so much. No matter how much dog breeding a dog owner does, his dogs will still be dogs.

Mutations cannot do what evolutionists say they can do.

A mutation *can* change existing genes, and thereby change (corrupt) the information of the DNA, but a mutation cannot add [new] information to DNA.

For example, a mutation can cause a cow to be born with an extra leg {you can do a search online to find pictures of this to show the class}**, but it cannot cause a cow to grow a turtle shell. The cow simply does not have the genetic material to produce a turtle shell. There are limits to how far an organism can change.**

Creationists would expect there to be [limits] to change within the various kinds of organisms. The observations of life around us indicate that there [are] limits to change.

Evolutionists would expect to see evidence of change from one major kind of organism to another. The evidence the evolutionists want is [not] there.

But the evolutionist still wants to say that mutations are responsible. Evolutionists don't seem to understand either the laws of genetics or the nature of mutations.

THE LAWS OF THE LEARNER APPLIED:

Having students debate will help fulfill the Law of Equipping, particularly the *Involve* step.

{Ask for a volunteer to come up in front of class to debate you on genetics and on the fossil record. You are the evolutionist; he is the Christian. You are to argue that mutations and natural selection explain the existence of all the kinds of animals. Argue as well that the fossil record proves evolution. The student should, with the help of his notes if necessary, show problems with evolution and give support to biblical creation. Take 4–5 minutes for this. If no student is willing to do this, have a student be the evolutionist.}

IV. THE YOUNG EARTH—THE EARTH ISN'T OLD ENOUGH FOR EVOLUTION.

{Write YOUNG EARTH on the board, introducing this as your fifth argument.}

As you know, evolutionists try to explain the existence of the universe apart from God. In

order to make the case for evolution, they need the earth to be very old. (Of course, as we have seen, even if the earth were billions of years old, evolution would still be impossible.) But there are many reasons to believe that the earth is young. Actually,

[90%] of the dating methods used to determine the age of the earth argue for a young earth.

For example,

The Young Faint Sun Paradox: Life could not have evolved on earth billions of years ago since the sun would have been fainter in the past and thus the earth would have been too [cold] for life.

{Draw on the board a sketch of the sun and earth.}

The sun is powered by nuclear reactions. Theoretically, the sun's core shrinks over time because of this, causing the nuclear reactions to occur more often. This means that over time the sun should burn brighter and brighter. This is no problem for a young earth. However, if the sun were old, there would be a major problem for evolution. Evolutionists believe that life appeared on the earth about 3.8 billion years ago. The sun would have been 25% fainter then, causing the earth to have an average temperature below freezing.

I'll share with you a couple more arguments for a young earth. {See www.answersingenesis.org/go/young for more information.}

Red blood cells and hemoglobin have been found in some [dinosaur] bones.

"But these could not last more than a few thousand years—certainly not the 65 million years from when evolutionists think the last dinosaur lived."

The moon is slowly receding from earth at about [1½] inches per year.

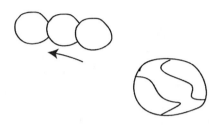

{Draw sketch of moon and earth; draw arrow signifying the moon's increasing distance from the earth.}

... and the rate would have been greater in the past. But even if the moon had started receding from being in contact with the earth, how long do you think it would have taken to reach its present distance of 239,000 miles? {Wait for response.} It would have taken about 1.37 billion years to reach its present distance. This gives a *maximum possible* age of the moon—not the *actual* age. This is far too young for evolution (and much younger than the radiometric "dates" assigned to moon rocks).

Salt is pouring into the sea much faster than it is escaping. The sea is not nearly salty enough for this to have been happening for [billions] of years.

"Even granting generous assumptions to evolutionists, the seas could not be more than 62 million years old—far younger than the billions of years believed by evolutionists. Again, this indicates a *maximum* age, not the *actual* age."

Arguments for a very old earth are based on unproven assumptions.

For example, radiometric dating "assumes that the rocks being analyzed have not been altered over time by migration of atoms in or out of the rocks, which requires detailed information from both the geological and chemical sciences. This is a huge assumption. Potassium and uranium, both common parent elements, are easily dissolved in water, so could be leached out of rocks. Argon, produced by decay from potassium, is a gas, so moves quite readily."

{Have students break into pairs. Have one be the atheist and the other be the Christian. Have the Christian make a case for creation using arguments for a young earth.}

V.   QUESTIONS FOR EVOLUTIONISTS

Before we close this lesson, I want to give you a list of questions you can use with evolutionists. These are questions that evolutionists have a hard time answering—because evolution is not an adequate explanation of reality. Asking these questions might help them really think about what they believe—and question it.

{Encourage the students to respond to these questions. Go around the room and have students read a few of the questions out loud. Give students the opportunity to respond like an evolutionist/atheist might to some of the questions.}

Ask the evolutionist:

1. How do you explain symmetry? Why does the human body have two arms on either side of the body, two eyes on either side of the face, two ears on either side of the head, etc.? Why are so many things almost perfectly proportioned?

2. How did emotions evolve? How did love evolve?

3. How did skin evolve?

4. How do you explain the evolution of teeth, eyes, and ears?

5. How did higher thinking evolve?

6. How did the process of photosynthesis evolve?

7. Which evolved first, the plants or the insects that live on and pollinate the plants?

8. Can you give me an example of a mutation that has added new information to the genome of an organism?

9. How do you explain the origin of the first living cell from non-living matter?

10. Why do some evolutionists who realize that life could not have come from non-life on this planet suggest that life was transported from another planet—when they know they are just moving the problem to another part of the universe?

11. If chance requires an average of 10 billion attempts to count from 1–10, and an average of 8.3 hundred quadrillion quadrillion attempts to spell "the theory of evolution," how in the world could chance ever produce even the simplest living cell, which is billions of times more complex?

12. Do you really believe that everything came from nothing?

13. If you believe that matter/energy has always existed, how do you deal with the Laws of Thermodynamics which say that there is a set amount of energy in the universe, but that this energy is becoming more and more unusable? Would the universe not have run down by now?

14. Which is easier to believe, "In the beginning God" or "In the beginning hydrogen"?

15. Why do you insist that the earth is so old, when 90% of dating methods suggest that the earth is relatively young?

16. Are you sure your answers are reasonable, right, and scientifically provable, or do you just believe that it may have happened the way you have answered?

{Have students break up into pairs and ask some of these questions of his or her "evolutionist" partner. Have the "evolutionist" try to answer these questions.}

VI. CONCLUSION

In this lesson, we have talked about the evolutionists' contradiction of:

The Law of Biogenesis

The Laws of Probability

The Laws of Thermodynamics

The Principles of Genetics

The Fossil Record

Scientific Evidence for a Young Earth

We have seen that evolutionists are not consistent with the facts of science. Their predictions do not hold up. They expect to see evidence that life could come from non-life; they expect time and chance to be capable of producing complexity; they expect mutations to explain evolution from single-celled organisms to man; and they expect to find transitional forms between major kinds of plants and animals. Yet their expectations are not fulfilled. Evolutionists contradict the laws of probability; they contradict the laws of thermodynamics; they contradict genetic laws; they contradict the fossil record; and they contradict the evidence for a young earth. They are unable to answer the tough questions about their theory—because their theory does not "hold water."

Atheistic evolutionists seem disconnected with reality, since they persist in their beliefs despite all the evidence to the contrary. And those who believe that God used evolution have compromised with man's theories about the age of the earth and evolution, while ignoring the clear teachings of the Bible.

The evidence from the world around us clearly supports a belief in God and creation rather than in evolution. The expectations of the creationist are easily supported by scientific research. Christians realize that life must come from life, and that ultimately our physical life (and spiritual life) comes from the One who is the Way, the Truth, and the Life. We realize that we could not have come into existence by chance. We believe in the Master Designer. We accept the laws of thermodynamics and the principles of genetics. These are not contradictory to our beliefs. The fossil record is consistent with our belief that God created everything according to its kind. Though we did not talk about the Genesis Flood in this lesson, we can say that the fossil record is consistent with a global Flood during Noah's time. We believe that the Bible teaches that the earth is relatively young; so the evidence for a young earth does not trouble us. Creationists have both God and science on their side! (I guess you would expect that God and science would be in agreement, since God is the God of all truth.)

You may have some friends or family members who have been convinced that evolution is true. I want you to share some of this information with them. With the Holy Spirit's help, you may persuade them to accept the truth about God's great creation.

{Do this activity if there is time. To help the students remember the key terms of the lesson, have students think of a concrete word to go with each of the terms (one association for each key term is suggested below). Then have students associate each word with the next.

Biogenesis (mouse)

Probability (coin)

Thermodynamics (running)

Genetics (dog)

Fossils (dinosaur)

Young earth (sun)

THE LAWS OF THE LEARNER APPLIED:

This use of mnemonics is a Law of Retention activity.

Write words in parentheses on board (and/or words that students choose). Review associations for each word, and then make up a sentence like the following: The *mouse*, which had a *coin* in its mouth, was *running* away from the *dog* when it was eaten by the *dinosaur,* which became extinct because of the hot *sun.*

Have students recall the lesson concepts by using the word associations. Quiz them verbally.}

I am going to send home with you a fascinating article on what is called the "Golden Ratio." The Golden Ratio is amazing evidence for design in the world. You could make this article part of your discussion with an evolutionist.

{Send home with students a copy of the article on the Golden Ratio, found in the Supplemental section for this lesson. Tell them to read it before the next class. If you have time, briefly discuss the article.}

APPLICATION:

Think of someone you know that has questions about this issue of origins (this may be someone on the list you made after the last class). Track that person down and ask him or her if you could share some of the information you learned in this lesson. If the person tends to believe in evolution, ask him or her questions from the last section of this lesson. Bring back to class a report of your interaction with this person.

6 THE GENERAL ARGUMENT FOR CHRISTIANITY

{Follow up on the class assignment from last week. Talk about the discussions that the class members had with skeptical friends, acquaintances, or family members. Total time: 5 minutes}

I hope you don't feel too old to play with blocks, because today we are going to use them to build a case for Christianity. How many of you think that it is important to give people a good explanation of why you are a Christian?

{Wait for response.}

What do you tell people when they ask you why you are a Christian? There's a story of a Mormon and a Methodist who were sharing with each other why they believed what they believed. The Mormon asked the Methodist, "Why are you a Methodist?" The Methodist responded, "I am a Methodist because I was born a Methodist, my father was born a Methodist, and his father was born a Methodist." "Why, that's smart," the Mormon scoffed, "What if you were born an idiot?" The Methodist said, "Then I would be a Mormon." {Pause.} The Methodist was not ready with a good answer for his faith, nor did he respond with gentleness and respect. Is that the way we should defend our faith? Is the only reason you can give for being a Christian that you were raised a Christian, or do you have a better argument?

These blocks today are going to help us present a *good* argument for Christianity. With them we are going to demonstrate that the Bible is the Word of God and that Jesus is the only way to God. But before we do that, I want to share with you an argument for the inspiration of Scripture that John Wesley used. I think you will like it.

He argued that "the Bible must be the invention of either good men or angels, bad men or devils, or of God.

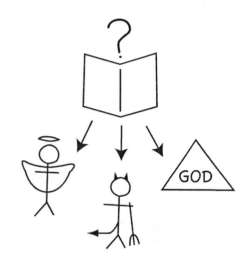

1. It could not be the invention of good men or angels, for they neither would nor could make a book, and tell lies all the time they were writing it, saying, 'Thus saith the Lord,' when it was their own invention.

2. It could not be the invention of bad men or devils, for they would not make a book which commands all duty, forbids all sin, and condemns their souls to Hell for all eternity.

3. Therefore I draw this conclusion, that the Bible must be given by divine inspiration."

There are other arguments for the inspiration of Scripture I do not recommend. One is a circular argument: Someone could ask: "Why do you believe the Bible is God's Word?" You could say, "Because, unlike any other book, every word in it is true." "But how do you know every word in it is true?" "Because it is God's Word." {Diagram this. Show how the argument is circular. Keep going around the circle until the students "get it."}

Do you see how this argues in a circle? It is the same as saying, like evolutionists, "The rocks date the fossils, and the fossils date the rocks."

The fossils date the rocks

The rocks date the fossils

What we need is a non-circular argument for the inspiration of Scripture and the truth of Christianity. It won't do you a whole lot of good to present arguments that are illogical—hardly anyone will accept them. You want to convince skeptics to become Christians, don't you? How would *you* argue that the Bible is the Word of God?

{Ask the students to try to refute you, the "skeptic." Tell them you don't believe the Bible. Have them respond. This activity may show them that they could use a better argument.}

Let's go to our blocks for some help. These blocks will allow us to build a case for Christianity that is logical and convincing. With these blocks we will demonstrate that the Bible is the Word of God, Jesus is the only way to Heaven, and that Christianity is true—without using circular reasoning.

{Present the argument for Christianity using 16-inch long wooden two-by-fours. These blocks will have key words on them to show how the case for Christianity is built. The *first block* will read: THE N.T. IS HISTORICALLY RELIABLE. (The capitalized words will appear on the blocks, not the marker board.) This block will lie flat on the table. Place the second two blocks on the foundational block.

The *second and third blocks* will read: RESURRECTION and PROPHECY. These two blocks will stand on end on either end of the foundation.

The *fourth block* will read: JESUS IS GOD. It will rest on the two blocks standing on end.

The *fifth block* will read: JESUS IS INFALLIBLE. This block will stand on its end in the middle of the structure already in place. On one of the wide sides of this fifth block, write: JESUS SAID THE BIBLE IS THE WORD OF GOD, and on the other wide side put: JESUS CLAIMED TO BE THE ONLY WAY.

One of the narrow sides of the *sixth block* will read: THE BIBLE IS THE WORD OF GOD; the other side

CHRISTIANITY IS TRUE
JESUS IS INFALLIBLE
JESUS IS GOD
PROPHECY
RESURRECTION
THE N.T. IS HISTORICALLY RELIABLE

will read: JESUS IS THE ONLY WAY. This block will be placed on the top of the previous block—on its end, so that the last two blocks form a "t." You can discuss the cross and the empty tomb, since you have a "t," which looks like a cross and an open space under it, which represents the empty tomb. On the very top of the structure (wide part), write: CHRISTIANITY IS TRUE. Place the appropriate blocks down as you quickly go through the following monologue. Wait to have the students fill in the blanks to the premises until after you go through the argument with the blocks.}

Let's see if we can build a case for Christianity. This first block represents the historical reliability of the Bible. This is the foundation. If the Bible is not at least generally reliable in its history, we have nothing to stand on. But since the N.T. is historically accurate, we have sufficient evidence to believe that Jesus rose from the dead and fulfilled many Messianic prophecies. These two pillars demonstrate that Jesus was who He said He was—the Messiah, God come in the flesh. Jesus is God. Since He is God, He is infallible. As an infallible authority, Jesus said that the Bible was the Word of God and that He was the only way to God. {Turn the block as you point this out.} **He cannot be wrong. Therefore, we conclude that the Bible *is* the Word of God and that Jesus *is* the only way to God. This means that Christianity is true!** {Turn the top block toward the class so they can see: CHRISTIANITY IS TRUE. Pause for effect, after having reached your conclusion with dramatic flair.} **Did you see what the top of this edifice looks like?** {Pause for response.} **Yes, a cross. This is the central message of Christianity, that God became flesh to die on the cross and rise from the tomb** {Make a sweeping motion out of the empty space underneath the cross, since this represents the empty tomb.} **so that we could be forgiven and reconciled to God.**

I'm going to have some of you come up and present the case for Christianity, using these blocks, but first let's fill in the blanks on our

THE LAWS OF THE LEARNER APPLIED:

The six blocks that "build" the case for Christianity will make the case for Christianity very concrete—solid. The need will be built through the objects (blocks) and the action of putting them together. The objects will also help the students remember. And since the students will be working with the blocks to practice convincing others, then the law of equipping is used as well.

outline. We will spend several weeks learning how to prove the premises of this argument. The important thing today is that we learn how the basic argument fits together.

{Now, go through the premises with the students. Wait to look up the Scriptures until this outline comes up again at the end of the elective.}

IS THE BIBLE THE WORD OF GOD AND JESUS THE ONLY WAY TO HEAVEN?

Premise A: The New Testament is historically accurate; it is a basically [reliable] and trustworthy document.

Again, this is the foundation; we need to build our case for the inspiration of Scripture on the fact that the New Testament documents in particular are historically accurate. If they are not accurate, we do not have a case; if they are, we can argue strongly for the validity of Christianity.

Premise B: On the basis of this reliable document, we have sufficient evidence to believe that Jesus [rose] from the dead as He predicted He would, and that He fulfilled dozens of other Messianic prophecies.

During the time of this course, we will have lessons on the Resurrection and fulfilled prophecy. We will show that premise B is definitely true.

Premise C: Jesus' Resurrection and fulfillment of prophecy show that He was who He said He was: the [Messiah], the Son of God—[God] in the flesh.

Premise D: Because Jesus is God, He is [infallible]—What He says is absolutely trustworthy.

Premise E: Jesus Christ taught that the Bible was the [Word of God] (Matt. 5:18, 15:4; Mark 12:36; Luke 24:44–46). He also taught that He was the only way to God (John 14:6).

{You will look up these Scriptures later.}

Conclusion: If Christ said it, we must believe it—The Bible is the Word of [God], and Jesus is the only way to God. Therefore Christianity is true.

What have we just done?! {Pause for response.} **We have shown that Christianity is true!**

If each of the premises above are true, the conclusion must be true. You notice how they build on one another, starting with the historical reliability of the Bible.[1]

{Have someone come up to challenge you. Make the statement that you believe that the Bible is the Word of God. Your challenger will ask why you think so. Point to the 2nd block down and say, "Jesus called the Bible divine. He said it was the Word of God." Your challenger will object to that by questioning why you simply accept Jesus' word for it. You point to the next block down and say, "Well, Jesus is infallible, therefore if He says the Bible is divine, then it is." Your challenger will say, "Why do you think Jesus is infallible?" You will point to the next block down and say, "Because He is God. If anybody is infallible, certainly God is." Then the challenger will question the deity of Christ. You will point to the next blocks down and say, "Fulfilled prophecy and the Resurrection of Christ show that He was who He said He was—God come in the flesh." When you are questioned concerning the Resurrection and prophecy, point to the first block and say, "The New Testament has been proven through science, archaeology, and historical research to be a completely reliable source of history. Since this is true, there is no reason to doubt the fact of the Resurrection and fulfilled prophecy." Have your "challenger" "convert" to Christianity.}

{Have your new "convert" help you convince a different person that *Jesus is the only way* (you will use the other side of the top two blocks), using the same technique. Have him do most of the responding. Help him when necessary. The other students will take notes.}

{Now have your original "convert" publicly persuade another person to "become a Christian," this time without your help. In front of the class, give him commendation and suggestions when he is done. Encourage him to keep using the arguments.}

{Now have the whole class pair up and quickly demonstrate to each other that Jesus is the only way to God and that the Bible is the Word of God. They will build the case for Christianity on paper, by drawing blocks. For the blocks that have more than one statement on them, they can write the minor points along the side. While the rest are practicing on paper, have a couple students come up front to "play" with the blocks, putting them together while presenting the argument.}

{Now come back and present the argument in 45 seconds. Have someone keep time. Make sure that the argument flows logically as you build with the blocks. Then have students come up and try to beat your time. If they do not present the argument with all the logical connections, let them know in front of the class so that the next person can do better. When a student does it more quickly than you, go through the presentation again yourself more quickly. Try to beat your students. Then they will try to beat you. Go back and forth. Then quit when you're ahead.}

But what if someone really gets tough and refuses to accept the idea that the New Testament is reliable? What if they say things like: "Well, the Bible has been copied over and over so many times that we don't know what was originally written." Or, "The stories in the New Testament are myths because they slowly developed over time. The original events were nothing like the records we have of them in the New Testament." Would you be able to

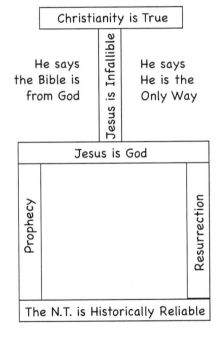

respond? These are common objections to the historical reliability of the New Testament. It is not enough just to know this general argument. You will need to know how to demonstrate that the Bible is historically accurate. During our next class, you will learn how to show someone that the Bible is historically reliable.

APPLICATION OF LESSON:

This week, find an unbeliever who will let you share with him the general argument for Christianity. Draw the blocks on paper, write in the premises, and verbally make the logical connections as you present the argument. If he says he believes something different, ask questions such as: What evidence do you have for that? Where did you learn that? What happens if you're wrong?

THE LAWS OF THE LEARNER APPLIED:

The application of the lesson will be the *Master* step of the Retention Method. It will also be the *Improve* step of the Equipping Method if the teacher takes the time to see how the students have done.

{Warn students about arguing with skeptics. Tell them that we should try to avoid the sense of competition that will make the skeptic feel that if he admits he is convinced, he has lost the argument. If possible, tell students a story about someone whom you shared this information with.}

NOTES

[1] You might point out to the students that, in starting our argument with the historical reliability of the N.T. instead of starting with the existence of God, we are assuming that the person we are talking to is open to a belief in an intelligent, holy God (Less than 10% of Americans claim to be atheistic). Tell the students that if they talk to someone lacking faith in the existence of God, they will want to share the information from Lessons 3–5.

7 THE RELIABILITY OF THE N.T.—BIBLIOGRAPHICAL TEST

{You may need to spend two weeks on this lesson.}

{Review the previous argument. Check on how the students did with their homework. Practice more with the blocks.}

We have just presented the general argument for Christianity. Now we have to demonstrate that each of the premises are true. If they are true, the conclusion will be true. But we have to *show* that they are true, beginning with the first premise.

There is a story about a business man walking down the street who noticed a blind man, who was wearing dark glasses, begging on a street corner. The business man tossed a few coins into the blind man's cup and walked away. However, he happened to glance back a few seconds later. What he saw made him angry. The "blind man" had pulled the glasses up to the top of his head and was peering down into the cup, evidently observing how much money the business man had given. The business man complained, "I thought you were supposed to be blind!" The "blind man" said, "Well, I'm not really; the blind man is on vacation, and I am taking his place. I'm usually the deaf and dumb person the next block over." {Pause.} **Why do scoundrels like this think they can get away with this kind of business? Because they know how gullible some people are. They know that some will believe their stories. Is it good to have a certain degree of skepticism when evaluating the character of people? What about the character of religions?** {Wait for response.} *Especially* **religions, since our decisions regarding religion will determine where we will spend eternity. We must not naively accept a religion just because a person advocating that religion sounds convincing.**

We must have objective evidence to demonstrate that a religion is true. Do we have proof that Christianity is true, or have we naively accepted a lie? I know that last time we met we made a case for Christianity using these blocks, but remember, we didn't prove that the N.T. is historically reliable. What would happen to our case for Christianity if someone proved that the N.T. was NOT historically reliable? {Wait for response.} **All of us would be proven to be gullible followers of a false religion.**

The Book of Mormon is not at all historically accurate, yet the Mormons accept it, proving themselves to be followers of a false religion. What about the New Testament? Maybe we had better check this out. Is the N.T. historically accurate or not?

{Divide the students into groups of four. Have two of each group be the "skeptics" and two the "apologists." Only have the "skeptics" open their student notes. On the notes are three objections to the historical reliability of the N.T. The "skeptics" will use these objections to question the "apologists" about the reliability of the N.T. The "apologists" will do their best to answer the questions, without seeing the notes. Let the possible frustration that comes from not knowing the most adequate answer help build the need for the material ahead. This activity should last about 3 minutes.}

THE LAWS OF THE LEARNER APPLIED:

The story and the questions that followed build the need by getting the students to think: "I don't want to appear gullible; I want to be able to show that what I believe is accurate. I want to know the evidence that the N.T. is reliable." The dialogues among the foursomes will build the need for the material by helping the student feel the gap between what he knows and what he should know.

How did you apologists do? If you found that your answers were a little weak, this class should help improve your ability to give answer questions like these.

Let me explain the first objection a little better; then we'll respond.

Objection 1: The N.T. was written 100–200 years after the life of Christ. How do we know we don't have a distorted picture of his life due to this gap?

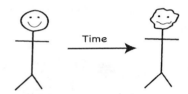

Doesn't it seem that if the N.T. were written 100–200 years after the life of Christ, we probably would not get an accurate picture of who He really was? {Pause briefly for response.} If an event were not recorded for that long, how could we trust the record of it?

{Draw two pictures of a face that becomes distorted after time passes.}

Do you see the problem? If there were a long oral tradition about Jesus, over time the original message about Jesus would have been greatly distorted, wouldn't it?

Fortunately, we don't have this problem. This objection is not valid at all because there is strong evidence that the N.T. was written during the eyewitness period—it was written during the time that there were still people around who actually witnessed the events described in the N.T. There was no time for myth to develop.

The N.T. was written within [60] (most books within 30) years of the death of Christ (AD 30).

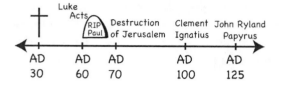

{As you present the evidence, show it on a timeline, showing how the dates of evidences keep getting farther and farther back to the original events.}

EVIDENCE:

1. [MANUSCRIPTS] have been found that date within or close to the first century:

    One Example: JOHN RYLAND PAPYRUS (dated **AD 125;** fragment of John found in Egypt). The original manuscript must have been written earlier.

THE LAWS OF THE LEARNER APPLIED:

The timeline with the pictures build the need and help the students remember the material. The students are also equipped because they are given a way to illustrate the concept that the N.T. was written within the eyewitness period.

{You can search online for pictures of the John Ryland Papyrus to show the class.}

2. Early church fathers (CLEMENT, IGNATIUS) were [quoting] many of the N.T. books by around **AD 100.** The books that were quoted had to be in circulation at that time.

3. There is no hint that the N.T. writers knew of the DESTRUCTION OF [JERUSALEM] **(AD 70)** as a fact that had already happened.

{Show picture of Herodian Jerusalem, Supplemental section.}

4. According to history, PAUL died in the **AD mid-[60s].**[1] At the end of Acts he is still alive. Therefore, Acts and the books Paul wrote most likely were written by the mid-60's. Luke wrote the book of Luke before he wrote the sequel, Acts. So the book of Luke is even earlier.

{Draw tombstone of Paul on the timeline at the appropriate date.}

Conclusion: There was not time for [myth] to grow up around the life of Christ.

Skeptics will have to think of another way that the life of Christ could be a myth. It certainly could not be because there is too much time between the events and the record of the events. The objection we have just answered has no validity whatsoever, even though it has been prevalent.

We have determined the approximate time that the N.T. was written, but we haven't determined whether it is historically reliable. For instance, how do we know that we have what was originally written? If we don't have what was originally written, then we can't trust the N.T.

If you want to determine whether or not the N.T. is reliable, you will need to use the three major tests that are used on every ancient document to determine its reliability. These three tests are used on any ancient piece of literature, such as Greek and Roman literature.

These three tests are 1. The BIBLIOGRAPHICAL Test, 2. The INTERNAL EVIDENCE Test, and 3. The EXTERNAL EVIDENCE Test. I will explain these tests as we apply them to the N.T. Once you know them and you are able to apply them to the Bible, you will easily answer people who have problems with the reliability of the N.T.

{One way that you can get the students to remember these tests is through the acronym B.I.E. Write it on the board. Say that you will not "B.I.E." their belief in the Bible unless it passes the Bibliographical Test, the Internal Evidence Test, and the External Evidence Test.}

Now let's actually get into the Bibliographical Test:

I. THE BIBLIOGRAPHICAL TEST

The BIBLIOGRAPHICAL TEST evaluates the reliability of manuscripts, looking at the [TIMESPAN] between original and existing manuscripts, [NUMBER] of manuscripts, and [QUALITY] (how much variation between the readings of the existing manuscripts). This test determines how well a document has been preserved since it was written. This test will determine whether or not we have what was originally written.

In a minute we are going to see how this test deals with a couple objections by skeptics. But before we look at the objections, let's make sure we know what these tests are.

What are the three tests to determine the reliability of an ancient document?

{Have class answer together: Bibliographical, Internal, External}

Again: {Have students repeat.}

What are the three aspects of the Bibliographical Test?

{Have class answer together: "time span, number, quality;" repeat.}

What does the Bibliographical Test do?

{Have a student answer. The Bibliographical Test determines how well a document has been preserved since it was written. It determines whether or not we have what was originally written.}

What does "timespan" mean?

{Have a student answer. The timespan refers to the number of years between the time an ancient document was written and the earliest surviving manuscripts (handwritten copies) of it.}

What does "number" mean?

{Have a student answer. Number refers to the number of existing handwritten copies of the ancient document.}

What does "quality" mean?

Objection 2: We do not have what was originally written because there is **too much time** between the original manuscripts and the earliest surviving copies. More time=more copying=more mistakes, and we don't even know what mistakes were made.

A. TIMESPAN

The timespan (between the originals and the earliest existing copies) for most classical Greek works is about 1,000 years; the time span for most books in the N.T. is around [90] years.

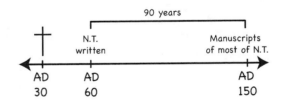

{Have a student answer. Quality refers to how similar all the existing manuscripts are. This aspect of the Bibliographical Test discusses how many differences there are between the handwritten copies we possess today.}

We have determined *when* the N.T. was written, but do we *have* what was originally written? That is what this next objection questions. How would you respond to it?

The Bibliographical Test will determine whether this objection is valid. Just looking at the timespan aspect of the Bibliographical Test will help us here.

{Draw a timeline with AD 60 marked as an average date for the writing of the N.T. Mark AD 150 as the general date by which we have whole manuscripts of most N.T. books. Show the timespan. Compare with other literature, using the chart below.}

Examples of manuscripts: The John Ryland Papyrus we already mentioned. Others are the CHESTER BEATTY PAPYRI (dated 120–150). {Put this on the timeline.} **These contain most of Paul's letters, the Gospels, and Acts.**

{Show the chart of the classical Greek works, comparing their timespans with that of the N.T. (in Supplementary section). Have them fill in the blanks in the chart that appears in their student notes.}

Author/Work	Timespan
Aristotle	1,400 yrs.
Tacitus	[1,000] yrs.
Caesar	950 yrs.
Odyssey	500 yrs.
New Testament	[90] yrs.

We don't think the classical literature was significantly corrupted; why should we think that the N.T. was corrupted during the 90-year span?

30 yrs. between events & writing

90 yrs. between originals & copies

N.T. written — Manuscripts of most of N.T.

AD 30   AD 60   AD 150

Objection 3: Even if there is a short time between the originals and the first copies, there are still **too many differences** among the surviving N.T. manuscripts for us to know what was in the original. All the copying over the years resulted in a huge number of conflicting manuscripts!

Can you see how well the N.T. passes this part of the test?

What is exasperating is that there is a double standard. Skeptics accept other ancient documents as reliable and reject the N.T. as unreliable even though the N.T. passes the tests for reliability much better than the other ancient documents. The inconsistency of the skeptics needs to be confronted.

What is the difference between the time period of this last objection and the period of the first one that we presented today?

{Have students respond. In the first objection, the period refers to the amount of time between the events and the written record of the events. In the second objection the period refers to the timespan between the written record and the earliest surviving manuscripts. Show the difference using a timeline.}

This is a very common objection to the reliability of the N.T. This argument is used often to suggest that we cannot trust the Bible and

therefore need something else besides it to guide us. The Mormons use this objection and say we need the Book of Mormon. The Muslims use this objection and say we need the Koran. How can we respond to this?

{Ask for a couple of volunteers to come up to the front of class together. Ask them (as a team) to respond to this objection. You are the skeptic. Afterwards, compliment them for their ability to respond as well as they did.}

With a little bit more information, we can refute this objection soundly. We must point the skeptic to the Number and Quality aspects of the Bibliographical Test.

B. NUMBER

The more manuscripts we have for comparison, the closer we can get to the original manuscript reading.

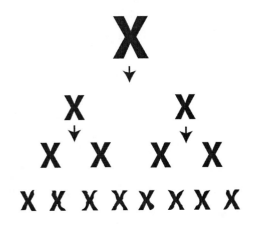

What is better, to have more manuscripts or fewer? {Wait for response.} Why more?

{Draw the "x's" to the left on the board. The large one represents the original documents; the others represent copies. The slight distortion to the "x's" on the bottom represents the small variations there are between later copies.}

The big "x" represents the original manuscripts; the small "x's" represent the copies. Since we no longer have the original set of manuscripts, we must depend on the copies to discover what was originally written. {Circle a few "x's" to represent those copies that still exist.} Since the existing copies would evidence different errors in copying (this is represented by the different shapes of the bottom "x's"), the best way to reconstruct the original is to compare as many manuscripts as possible. If a great variety of manuscripts are analyzed, we can be sure that whatever all the copies agree on was in the original manuscripts. With a great number of manuscripts, we can also be confident that somewhere among all the

manuscripts the original form of every passage is present. Is there that much manuscript evidence for the N.T.?

5,700—Greek

10,000—Latin

9,300—other versions

──────────

[25,000] total manuscripts, fragments

Plus tens of thousands of quotations from the N.T. by the early church fathers.

The quantity of manuscripts of classical Greek and Roman literature is very small. The piece of ancient literature (besides the Bible) with the greatest quantity of existing manuscripts is Homer's [Iliad] (643 copies). The manuscript evidence for the N.T. is far superior to the manuscript evidence of classical Greek and Roman literature!

{Show a chart comparing a few pieces of Roman and Greek literature with the Bible concerning the number of existing manuscripts—Supplemental section.}

Author/Work	# of Copies
Plato	7
Caesar	10
Tacitus	20
Homer	643
New Testament	5,700 (Greek)

"The number of [manuscripts] of the N.T., of early [translations] from it, and of [quotations] from it in the oldest writers of the church, is so large that it is practically certain that the true reading of every doubtful passage is preserved in some or other of these ancient authorities. **This can be**

Do we have the original N.T.?

☐ No change
☐ Spelling & grammar changes
☐ Significant changes

said of no other ancient book in the world." (Frederick Kenyon, renowned paleographer[2] and textual critic)

C. QUALITY

{Draw or present the pie chart of the Quality of the N.T. manuscripts; see previous page and Supplemental section. Explain that 7/8ths of the N.T. is the same in all of the manuscripts. Of the 1/8th that is left, most differences in the manuscripts are spelling, style, or grammar differences. Only about 1/8th of the 1/8th (or about 1/60th of the whole) are significant differences. In other words:}

About [400] differences are significant to the meaning of the N.T.[3] This is less than one per page in an English translation.

The N.T. is at least [98%] pure.

Compare that with the ancient Roman and Greek literature. Most pieces of literature cannot be reconstructed enough to know what percentage was in the original for sure. One exception is Homer's *Iliad*, with 643 copies. It is about 95% pure. The N.T., which is at least 98% pure, compares very well with other ancient literature.

In spite of errors in the copying, no variant reading harms any [doctrine] of the N.T. Though a disputed passage may touch on doctrine, every doctrine of the N.T. is taught in its indisputable parts.

Though these arguments do not *prove* that the Bible is the Word of God (we will get to that part later), they do confirm that we have what was originally written. If what was written is the Word of God, we have that same Word today. Assuming that the Bible is from God, we can say with Kenyon:

{Quote the following with intensity of voice and a Bible in your hand.}

"The Christian can take the whole Bible in his hand and say without fear or hesitation that he holds in it the true Word of God, handed down without essential [loss] from generation to generation throughout the centuries" (Frederick Kenyon).

The evidence more than suggests that we have what was originally written. There can be no doubt that we have essentially what the N.T. authors wrote in the middle of the first century AD.

{Review the three tests, and the three aspects of the bibliographical test as you did before. Then have the students get into groups of four. Two of the four will be "skeptics;" the other two "apologists." Give the "apologists" 5 minutes to prove to the "skeptics" that we know we have what was originally written. They should also demonstrate that the N.T. was written during the eyewitness period. They should draw the timeline and the pie chart. Listen to the conversations; offer critique when it is helpful. Encourage them to keep sharing this lesson with others. Announce that there will be a little quiz at the beginning of the next class to see how much they learned.}

II. APPLICATION OF LESSON

Talk to an unbeliever about the reliability of the N.T. Show him that Christians have what was originally written and that the N.T. was written within a generation of the events. Use the timeline and the pie chart. Report on your conversation next week in class.

NOTES

[1] In case students ask, the Roman emperor Nero died in AD 68. According to Eusebius, a church father, Paul died under the reign of Nero.

[2] A paleographer studies ancient manuscripts.

[3] The only textual variants which affect more than a sentence or two are John 7:53–8:11 (the story of the woman caught in adultery) and Mark 16:9–20 (the end of the book). Both of these passages were probably in the original manuscripts. Most variants affect only individual words or phrases.

$\mathcal{8}$ Historical Reliability of the N.T.—Internal & External Tests

{You may want to spend two weeks on this lesson.}

{At the beginning of class, give a quiz over Lesson 7; see Quiz Two in the Supplemental section. Discuss it briefly afterwards.}

{Review the three tests for the historical reliability of the N.T.—Bibliographical, Internal, and External Evidence. Have the words written on the board.}

What did we prove using the Bibliographical Test?

{Wait for answer, which is: we proved that what we have today in our New Testament is what was in the original manuscripts. Last time we also discussed why we believe that these original books were written within a generation of Jesus' lifetime.}

Did we demonstrate that what the authors wrote was accurate? {No.} We *have* what they *wrote*, but how do we know that they wrote *accurately*? How do we know that the N.T. writers were honest? Maybe they were making up a myth. Maybe it was a conspiracy to gain power or popularity. How can we know how accurate they were? We can know by looking at the **INTERNAL EVIDENCE** and the **EXTERNAL EVIDENCE**.

Is there anything we can tell about the writer's accuracy by simply looking at the writing itself? Yes. Looking for evidence this way is called the internal evidence test of the document. The internal evidence test analyzes what is written to determine whether we can trust the author.

I. INTERNAL EVIDENCE Test— Can we trust what the authors wrote?

Were they honest, competent?

A. The Benefit of the Doubt

We need to remember:

Aristotle's Dictum: "The benefit of the doubt is to be given to the [document] and not to the critic."

For example, if there is a possible explanation for a supposed contradiction in a document, the document should not be considered erroneous on the basis of that supposed contradiction.

B. Contradictions?

Are there contradictions in the Bible? How many of you have had someone tell you that there were?

{Wait for response. Maybe tell about someone you talked to.}

If there are, the contradictory statements must violate the law of non-contradiction in order for them to be real contradictions.

{Have a student read the next sentence, then you read the second sentence, filling in the blank.}

LAW OF NON-CONTRADICTION:

If one statement absolutely contradicts another statement, without qualification, at least one of those statements cannot be true.

But in order for one statement to absolutely contradict another, there must be no sense in which the statements can both be true. If there is a possible [logical] explanation, it is not a real contradiction.

Example: When was Christ crucified?

John 19   Mark 15

6ᵗʰ hour   3ʳᵈ hour

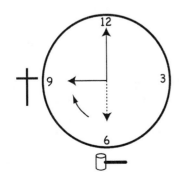

To illustrate: one Gospel says there was one angel at Jesus' tomb; another says there were two. Is there an absolute contradiction here? No, because the gospel that says there was one angel doesn't say there was *only* one. If it did, then that would be an absolute contradiction to the Gospel that says there were two.

{For maximum impact, act as if you found a real contradiction in the Bible. Say something like: "I think I did actually find a real contradiction in the Bible." Then say the following:}

JOHN 19 says that Jesus was standing before Pilate the 6TH HOUR. MARK 15 says that Jesus was crucified the 3RD HOUR.

{Under John 19, draw stick figure in front of throne. Under Mark 15, draw a cross; see below. Write below the throne: *6th hour*; write below the cross: *3rd hour*.}

How could He be standing before Pilate after He was crucified? It's a contradiction; isn't it?

{See if someone can figure out the solution.}

The solution is that John was in all likelihood using Roman time (like our time, counting time beginning at midnight and going through the next day), and Mark was using Jewish time (counting time beginning around 6:00 p.m. and *then again* around 6:00 a.m., sunrise).

{Draw a clock with appropriate markings on the board to illustrate. Draw a gavel by 6:00 a.m. and a cross by 9:00.}

This would mean that Jesus was standing before Pilate at 6:00 a.m. (6th hour Roman time) and was crucified at 9:00 a.m. (3rd hour Jewish time). It took Jesus three hours to get from

before Pilate to the Cross. This is a reasonable explanation.

A seminary student said to professor R.C. Sproul, author of *Reason to Believe*, "The Bible is full of contradictions." Sproul says that he responded like this, "The Bible is a large book. If it is full of contradictions you should have no problem finding 50 clear violations of the law of contradiction in the next 24 hours. Why don't you go home and write down 50 contradictions and we'll discuss them at the same time tomorrow." The student accepted the challenge. He returned bleary-eyed with 30, after having searched long into the night. He presented Sproul a list of the most blatant contradictions he could find (he had made use of critical books that listed such contradictions). Sproul says, "He went through his list, one at a time, applying the test of formal logic to each alleged contradiction. We used syllogisms, the laws of immediate inference, truth tables, and even Venn diagrams to test for logical inconsistency and contradictions. In every single incident we proved objectively, not only to my satisfaction, but to his, that not a single violation of the law of contradiction was made."[1]

Write this down: There are no proven absolute contradictions in the Bible.

In fact, the more we find out about science, history, and the Bible, the more supposed problems in the Bible are solved.

THE LAWS OF THE LEARNER APPLIED:

Acting like you found a contradiction in Scripture will stir the students' feelings ("build the need"). The story about Sproul and the student will heighten feelings for the subject of contradictions. It will give the students a stronger feeling of confidence concerning the defense of the Scripture.

The list of alleged discrepancies gets shorter and shorter.

{Diagram a list of discrepancies using long dashes on the board. As you say "shorter and shorter and shorter...," erase several of the dashes (one by one), leaving a much shorter list.}

It is interesting that in the case of the Book of Mormon, the list of discrepancies gets longer and longer. The longer it is studied, the more contradictions are found. In the case of the Bible, the longer it is studied, the more problems are resolved.

Plus, any surface "contradictions" that we do see actually help the case for the reliability of the N.T. Anybody know why? {Wait for response.} Because they show that the authors were truly writing from their own perspectives rather than scheming together to get their "story" right.[2] (This is especially important for the Resurrection narratives.)

C. The Authors Based Their Accounts on [EYEWITNESS] TESTIMONY.

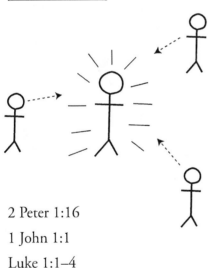

2 Peter 1:16

1 John 1:1

Luke 1:1–4

{Have the students look up the three passages in their notes. Each of these indicates that the writers were eyewitnesses or based their records on eyewitness testimony.}

{While the students are looking up the scriptures, sketch a person signifying Jesus. Draw three stick figures looking at him from different perspectives.}

It is obvious that the Gospels were based on the memories of people who had close contact with Jesus and a direct knowledge of what happened. Since the disciples' time with Jesus would have been so significant to them, they would most likely have remembered the details well. In fact, Jesus told His disciples that the Holy Spirit would bring to their remembrance all that He had said to them (John 14:25–26).

This confirms their recall [ability].

D. Contemporary Critics Were a Constant Corrective.

The authors no doubt tried to be very careful with how they handled the facts. During the time they wrote, they had a lot of [critics] who would have loved to discredit their testimony. If the authors had made a mistake, the critics would have pointed it out.

E. The Authors [Died] for Their Doctrine.

{Visualize with a sketch of a tombstone with Matthew's name on it. There is a scroll on top of the tombstone with a sword sticking into it.}

People will sometimes die for what they believe to be true, but never for something they *know* to be [false].

If the Resurrection had not taken place, the disciples would have known it.

The authors willingly gave their lives for their belief in Christ's Resurrection.

This confirms their [honesty].

Their willingness to die for their faith confirms what? {Wait for answer, which is their honesty.} **The fact that they based their stories on eyewitness testimony confirms what?** {Wait for answer, which is their ability.} **So it looks like the weight of the evidence favors the idea that the N.T. writers were honest and close enough to the facts to be able to present them accurately. They were both trustworthy and competent. We have internal evidence that we have a reliable N.T.**

THE LAWS OF THE LEARNER APPLIED:

This activity corresponds to the *Memorize* step of the Retention Method and the *Involve* and *Improve* steps of the Equipping Method.

II. The EXTERNAL EVIDENCE Test—Is There Outside Corroboration?

A. Supporting Evidence from Other Early Christian Writers

1. Papias, acquaintance of John the apostle: "The Elder [the Apostle John] used to say this also: 'Mark, having been the interpreter of [Peter], wrote down [accurately] all that he [Peter] mentioned, whether sayings or doings of Christ, not, however, in order.'"

Irenaeus, student of Polycarp (student of John):

> "So firm is the ground upon which these Gospels rest, that the very [heretics] themselves bear witness to them, and starting from these documents, each one of them endeavors to establish his own particular doctrine."

Even those in the early church who didn't respect apostolic doctrine still respected the Gospel records; the Gospels must have been considered extremely reliable documents in those days.

B. Supporting Evidence from Early Non-Christian Historical Sources.

What would we know about Christ and Christianity if we didn't have the Bible? Anything? Are

there any non-Christian sources that confirm what is presented in the N.T. as fact?

{Have two students be Pliny the Younger and Emperor Trajan. Pliny will read part of the letter he wrote to the Emperor while he (Pliny) was governor of Bithynia (in Asia Minor). This was about AD 112. Emperor Trajan will read his letter in response. They should read the letters in a dignified manner. Ask the class what they learned about Christ and the Christians from the exchange. See Supplemental section for letters.}

We get the following picture if we combine the testimonies of Josephus, Tacitus, Lucian, Suetonius, Pliny the Younger, Thallus, and the Talmud—all contemporary non-Christian sources:

1. Jesus was crucified under Pontius Pilate at Passover time. (Tacitus, Thallus, Josephus, Talmud)

{Draw a cross on the board.}

2. He was believed by his disciples to have risen from the dead three days later. (Josephus)

{Draw an empty tomb on the board.}

3. Jewish leaders charged Christ with [sorcery] and believed He was born of adultery. (Talmud)

What do these accusations suggest? {Wait for response.} **Christ was doing some astonishing things, and there was something unusual about His birth. These accusations actually allude to Christ's miracles and Virgin Birth.**

4. The Judean sect of Christianity spread even to [Rome]. (Tacitus, Suetonius)

5. [Nero] and other Roman rulers bitterly persecuted and martyred early Christians. (Tacitus, Suetonius)

6. Early Christians denied polytheism, lived dedicated lives according to Christ's teaching, and [worshiped] Christ. (Pliny, Lucian)[3]

We would know all of the above simply by reading secular and Jewish history. As you can see, there is outside confirmation that the N.T. is accurate historically. We will next see if archaeology confirms or disproves the N.T.

C. Archaeology as External Evidence

1. SIR WILLIAM RAMSAY

Sir William Ramsay was a well-known, highly-respected archaeologist.

He went to study in the Bible lands as a liberal; fifteen years later he became a firm believer in a reliable New Testament.

Ramsay was originally skeptical of the reliability of the N.T., and therefore he neglected to consult it for help in his research. But eventually he used the writings of Luke to study Asia Minor and was surprised at how reliable Luke was.

Ramsay said that [Luke] was unsurpassed as an historian.

For example, when Luke made reference to [32] countries, [54] cities, and [9] islands, he made no mistakes.

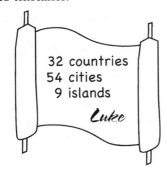

32 countries
54 cities
9 islands
Luke

{Present sketch of a scroll signed by Luke as above. Have students remember the numbers by pointing out that 3+2=5 and 5+4=9. Also, remember that *countries* come before *cities* because countries are larger than cities.}

2. The PAVEMENT

• The place where Jesus was tried before Pilate.

Near the Jaffa Gate in Jerusalem.

• Once considered a [myth] because there was no record of it in Jewish or secular maps or history.

• It was finally [found].

This is what had happened:

• When Titus destroyed Jerusalem, he built barracks there. When these were abandoned and had crumbled, other buildings were built on top. Archaeologists had dug down to the barracks, but no further until recently. When they did go underneath, they found the [pavement].

3. The POOL OF BETHESDA

• Mentioned in John 5, as the place Jesus healed an invalid.

{Read or quote from the first part of John 5. Point out that John said the pool of Bethesda had five porches, or colonnaded walkways.}

• No record in Jewish or secular maps or histories; therefore considered a [myth].

• In 1888, it was found while archaeologists were digging around the Church of [St. Anne].

It lies about forty feet below the ground.

Guess how many porches at the pool there is evidence of?

{Wait for response. There is evidence of five. The N.T. is repeatedly determined to be historically reliable. We don't ever have to worry about the archaeologists finding something that would disprove the accuracy of the Bible.}

{Show a picture of part of the excavated pool of Bethesda; see Supplemental section.}

This is just a little bit of the vast amount of archaeological evidence that supports the historicity of the N.T.

4. NELSON GLUECK*

{**ue* is pronounced as a short *e*.}

- Jewish, and universally esteemed as one of the greatest archaeologists.

- Said that no archaeological discovery has ever [contradicted] the Bible.

I am going to quickly ask some review questions. Let's see how much we remember. If we can remember what we talked about today, we will be armed to defend the N.T. when someone we are talking to has a problem with its reliability.

{Some of the questions can be answered in unison; some questions will be answered by volunteers; others will be answered by students you call on. The review time must move quickly; it should be no more than 5 minutes. Any pictures or diagrams that you can briefly show as you ask the questions will be helpful.}

1. **What do the Internal and External tests prove?**

2. **What is Aristotle's dictum?**

3. **What is the law of non-contradiction?**

4. **How many proven absolute contradictions are there in the Bible?**

5. **The Bible's list of alleged contradictions is getting _____; the Book of Mormon's list is getting _____.**

6. **Solve the problem of the timing of the Crucifixion: John says he was standing before Pilate the sixth hour; Mark says he was crucified the third hour.**

7. Give three reasons why we can trust the authors of the N.T. (apart from the absence of absolute contradictions).

8. What is one verse in the N.T. that indicates that the writers were eyewitnesses of Jesus or at least interviewed eyewitnesses? (verse and reference)

9. What did Papias (a church father who knew John the Apostle) say concerning Mark and Peter?

10. What are six things we know about Christ and Christianity from non-Christian sources?

11. Archaeologists say that when Luke made reference to _____ countries, _____ cities, and _____ islands, he made no mistake.

{Show sketch of the scroll, but erase the numbers.}

12. Use the "Pavement" and the "Pool" to prove that there is archeological support for the historical reliability of the N.T.

{Again show the picture of the Pool of Bethesda.}

13. The famous archaeologist Nelson Glueck believed that there were contradictions between the Bible and archaeology. (True or False)

We have shown today that the N.T. passes the internal evidence test and the external evidence test. Last time we showed that the N.T. passed the Bibliographical Test. These are the three tests that determine whether a document is historically reliable. What is our conclusion? That the N.T. is a trustworthy historical document.

Now let's go back to our blocks, confident that we have a solid foundation on which to build our case for Christianity!

{Bring out the blocks again, and quickly present the general argument for Christianity. Appoint a timekeeper. See if anyone wants to challenge your speed. After someone else builds the blocks, ask him why he is so sure that the N.T. is historically reliable. See how he responds. Compliment and critique accordingly.}

III. Application of Lesson

Share the internal and external evidence for the historical reliability of the N.T. with someone who has doubts. Use diagrams on paper as much as possible. If he says that he has problems with the N.T. because of contradictions, ask him, "What contradictions? Could you give me some examples?" Share an example of a contradiction that has been resolved.

NOTES

[1] R.C. Sproul, *Reason to Believe*, Zondervan, Grand Rapids, 25–26, 1982.

[2] There is amazing consistency among the writers concerning the overall picture and subtle details. Since this is true, the surface "contradictions" actually help the case for reliability. Between nine and ten writers were mostly writing independently when they testify to the life of Christ. The number of independent witnesses is a definite advantage of the N.T. over other ancient literature.

[3] For more information, read Josh McDowell and Bill Wilson, *He Walked Among Us*, Thomas Nelson, Nashville, 1993.

9 THE RESURRECTION OF JESUS CHRIST

{This lesson may need to be broken into 2 or 3 sessions. You may find it best to cover the first major section (under Roman numeral one) the first time you meet. Then you could finish the lesson the next time you meet.}

{Play a good Resurrection song (CD or cassette tape), such as "Because He Lives." The chorus should be played before the lesson starts, then the volume should be turned down so the class hears a verse or two and choruses as background music to the beginning of the teaching part of class.}

The Resurrection of Jesus is either the greatest hoax of all time or the most glorious marvel of all time. Christianity either stands or falls on the answer to the question: "Did the historical Jesus physically rise from the dead?" Paul said that if He didn't rise, our faith is vain, and we are a miserable people. Why would he say that? {Wait for response.} **Because if Christ did not rise, then we will not rise again ourselves. We would not have eternal life.**

The phenomenon of the Resurrection is central to the truth of Christianity. Is there evidence for this event in history? We'll talk about that today!

If we argue for the Resurrection, we need to first demonstrate that Jesus actually died. Then we can discuss whether or not He rose from the dead.

I. The Resurrection: At the HEART of the Gospel

By the way, we will remember the main arguments for the Resurrection with the acrostic HEART. The Resurrection is at the heart of the gospel and the heart of Christianity! And according to Romans 10, we must believe in our HEART that Jesus rose from the dead.

Horrible Death

We spent the last couple lessons showing you that the books of the N.T. are historically accurate. On the basis of these historically accurate documents, we have sufficient evidence to believe that Jesus actually died. We get the details of His death mostly from the Gospels.

1. Heavy loss of [blood]

Even before Jesus was crucified He lost a lot of blood. The Roman floggings were terribly brutal, much worse than a modern day flogging. I quote a medical doctor cited in *The Case for Christ*:

"Roman floggings ... usually consisted of thirty-nine lashes. ...The soldier would use a whip of braided leather thongs with metal balls woven into them. When the whip would strike the flesh, these balls would cause deep bruises or contusions, which would break open with further blows. And the whip had pieces of sharp bone as well, which would cut the flesh severely.

"The back would be so shredded that part of the spine was sometimes exposed by the deep, deep cuts. The whipping would have gone all the way from the shoulders down to the back, the buttocks, and the back of the legs. It was just terrible. ...One physician who has studied Roman beatings said, 'As the flogging continued, the lacerations would tear into the underlying skeletal muscles and produce quivering ribbons of bleeding flesh.' A third-century historian by the name of Eusebius described a flogging by saying, 'The sufferer's veins were laid bare, and the very muscles, sinews, and bowels of the victim were laid open to exposure.'"[1]

A person going through this would experience horrible pain and would lose a tremendous amount of blood. That is why Jesus collapsed on His way to the place of Crucifixion, and they had to find someone else to carry His cross. Jesus was already in critical condition even before He was hung on the Cross.

2. When His side was pierced, blood and water flowed out.

{Depict the Crucifixion with a diagram or picture—a person on a cross. Depict blood and water flowing out.}

After a person had been crucified, soldiers would thrust a spear into a victim's side to make sure he was dead. Physicians agree that blood and water flowing out is a sign of death. If Jesus was not dead, blood alone would have spurted out.

3. Soldiers didn't break His [legs].

Soldiers would break the legs of the crucifixion victims in order to speed up their deaths because it would be much harder to breathe if the victim couldn't push himself up. In the case of Jesus, when they came to him to break His legs, they didn't—because they knew He was already dead. And with their experience, they would have known whether someone was dead or not.

4. Pilate asked for [<u>assurance</u>] (from the centurion) that Jesus was dead.

5. He was wrapped completely in bandages and laid in a tomb.

{Sketch a tomb.}

No one was in doubt that Jesus was dead.

6. Non-Christian sources confirm the Crucifixion of Jesus.

Christ's death by crucifixion is acknowledged by Jewish and Roman historians. We mentioned this last time.

If the resurrection really did happen, then the body that was buried would vacate its tomb. Remember we're not talking about a spiritual resurrection (a non-physical resurrection of the spirit), but a bodily, physical resurrection. This is what Jesus predicted, and this is what the apostles later preached. Why is the bodily resurrection significant to apologetics (and whether or not the apostles told the truth)?

{Wait for response. Hint: It has to do with proving the Resurrection.}

If the disciples had wanted to deceive the world, it would have been much easier to teach a non-literal Resurrection, so there would be no need of proof for it. But instead, the disciples taught that Jesus literally, physically rose from the grave. This means that there would need to be real proof for the Resurrection. The tomb, for one thing, would have to be empty. Here is the evidence:

EMPTY TOMB

1. **The Jews through history have admitted that the tomb was empty. They only give reason for the tomb's vacancy— belief in the empty tomb is assumed.**

Trypho, a Jew, said in the second century:

> "One Jesus, a Galilean [deceiver], ... we crucified, but his disciples [stole] him by night from the tomb, where he laid when unfastened from the cross, and now deceive men by asserting that he has risen from the dead and ascended into heaven." (*Dialogue with Trypho*, by Justin Martyr)

2. **Christianity could not have originated in [Jerusalem] within a few weeks of the supposed Resurrection if there were no empty tomb.**

Why not? No one would have believed the Resurrection if there were no empty tomb, seeing the Resurrection was first preached in Jerusalem (the very city in which the body had lain) within a few [weeks] of the Crucifixion and burial.

3. **Other explanations for the empty tomb are not reasonable.**

Let's talk about three of the most popular explanations:

a. The disciples stole the body.

This is the theory that the unbelieving Jews came up with (see Matthew 28:11–15). Why isn't it a good explanation?

{Wait for response.}

The disciples would have had to sneak by or overpower the Roman guard outside the tomb.

If the disciples stole the body, they died for what they knew was a [lie].

Can we trust the apostles to have told the truth?

{Quickly draw on the board a symbol for each way an apostle was killed (according to the N.T. or tradition).}

Peter, crucified

Andrew, [crucified]

Matthew, by the sword

James, son of Alpheus, [crucified]

Philip, crucified

Simon, [crucified]

Thaddaeus, [killed by arrows]

James, brother of Jesus, stoned

Thomas, [spear thrust]

Bartholomew, crucified

James, son of Zebedee, [the sword]

> "Nothing in law so convinces courts and juries of the truthfulness of a story as the fact that a man's life has been [consistent] with such story" (Henry Barnett, attorney).

The apostles' lives (and deaths) were consistent with their testimony to the Resurrection.

b. Maybe the Jewish or [Roman] authorities removed the body.

But if they had removed it, they would have [produced] it for everyone to see. Why?

Why would they have produced the body?

{Wait for response.}

The Jews wanted to destroy what they thought was a heresy; the Romans wanted to keep the peace.

c.   [SWOON] THEORY

{Sketch an almost-dead person who revives slightly.}

More [incredible] than a Resurrection

Look back at the evidence for His death. After all that Jesus went through, how could He still be alive? Even if He hadn't died but had instead survived in an extremely weakened state, how could this wasted leader have rolled away a huge stone and then convinced His followers (after He survived the ordeal) that He was Lord of Life and Victor over death?

Since other options are not reasonable, we are left with the only option that makes sense—that Jesus rose just as He said He would. This certainly is the only option that fits in with the reports of the appearances of Jesus after the tomb was vacated.

What confirms the evidence of the empty tomb is the post-Resurrection appearances of Jesus.

APPEARANCES AFTER THE RESURRECTION

1. **In 1 Corinthians 15:3–8, Paul gives a list of some of those who saw Christ:**

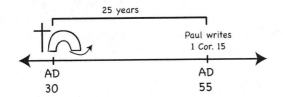

He wrote this list around AD 55, only 20–25 years after the Resurrection.

{Draw timeline, showing date of Crucifixion and date that Paul wrote 1 Corinthians.}

Peter

The Twelve

500 brethren at once, most still alive when Paul wrote this

Paul says in this passage that most of these 500 were still alive. Why would Paul mention these still-alive witnesses if the Resurrection hadn't happened? It seems like he was open to people challenging his word.

James

Paul himself

2. The Gospels also record the testimony of others who saw Christ after He had been crucified.

Some of these were Mary Magdalene and other women.

Why should we believe the testimony of these early Christians who said they saw Christ?

{Wait for response to this question. Make sure everyone is participating in responding to your class questions. You may have to call on some students that do not usually volunteer.}

These early Christians risked their lives for what they said they saw, and many died for their belief. If the Resurrection had not taken place, they would have known it and would not have died for what they knew was a lie.

RECORD OF WOMEN AS THE [FIRST] WITNESSES

The point is stronger than it might initially seem. Remember, we said that women were included among those who saw Jesus after He rose. They are actually identified as those who saw Jesus and the empty tomb first. What is the significance of this? {Wait for response.}

A woman's witness wasn't respected in court in those days; they were not legal witnesses—they had a lower social status. It seems that if the Gospel writers were making the story up, they would not have had the women be the first witnesses of the empty tomb and Jesus.

TRANSFORMATION OF DISCIPLES

Peter

He was transformed from a cowardly denier of Christ to a courageous proclaimer of the Resurrection.

Paul

The greatest antagonist of Christianity became its greatest advocate.

James, Jesus' brother

James was skeptical of his half-brother until the Resurrection; but afterwards he became the leader of the Jerusalem church.

Each of these apostles had nothing to gain if the Resurrection were false. They ended up giving their lives for their belief in the Resurrection.

{Write the letters H E A R T on the board. Review the main points using diagrams.}

Horrible Death

{Draw the Cross.}

Empty Tomb

{Draw the empty tomb next to the Cross.}

Appearances after Death and Burial

{Beside the empty tomb, draw a stick figure (that appears to be glowing) facing a few other stick figures (who represent those who saw Jesus).}

Record of Women as the First Witnesses

{Draw long hair on a couple of the witnesses and put "1st" above them.}

Transformation of Disciples

{Draw a curved arrow (180 degree turn) next to the stick figures who faced Jesus. This will represent the fact that the disciples' lives were changed after the Resurrection.}

{Have the students recite the main points with you until you are confident they know them.}

{Appoint someone to be timekeeper. Give yourself 120 seconds to present to the class the argument for the Resurrection, using the HEART acrostic. This is just a summary. Illustrate it. Then have a volunteer present this to the class with your help (you draw the pictures), in two minutes. Then have the student sit down. Have a second volunteer, in 120 seconds, present the argument to the class, drawing the pictures. Critique your volunteers and encourage them to keep using the arguments.}

{Have a student present the Resurrection argument from the HEART acrostic as another student draws the diagram on the board. Have yet another student keep time. The student must be finished in two minutes.}

II. What Happens When One Examines the Evidence Objectively?

Here are a couple examples of highly-educated skeptics who decided to look at the evidence for the Resurrection:

A. Simon Greenleaf—professor of law at Harvard in the 1800s

His three-volume work *A Treatise on the Law of Evidence* has been considered by the Supreme Court to be the greatest single authority on legal evidence.

Greenleaf was a Jew, not a Christian. But his Christian students challenged him to look at the evidence for the Resurrection of Jesus from a lawyer's perspective. He did and became a Christian.

He said, "If the evidence for the resurrection was set before any unbiased courtroom in the world it would be judged to be an historical [fact]— Jesus Christ rose from the dead!"

He wrote an apologetics book called *The Testimony of the Evangelists.*

{Show the book to the students if you have it.}

B. Lord Lyttleton and Gilbert West, friends at Oxford

Lyttleton tried to prove Saul was never converted.

West tried to prove Christ never rose from the dead.

They separated to look at the evidence independently. They planned to come back together to write a book refuting Christianity.

What happened after each independently looked at the evidence and came back together?

They each independently became Christians after looking at the unsurmountable evidence for the truthfulness of Christianity. When they conferred, each discovered that the other had become a Christian.

These are just two of many examples of people who have tried to look objectively at the evidence and have been convinced of the truth of the Resurrection, even if they were previously prejudiced against the Resurrection.

III. Other Evidence for the Resurrection

Now we will briefly discuss some of the other Resurrection arguments that helped Greenleaf, Lyttleton, West, and many others to become convinced Christians. Then we are going to set up for a Resurrection trial!

We can remember these arguments for the Resurrection with the acrostic WE ARGUE. We argue for the Resurrection with the following facts. These facts can not stand alone as evidence for the Resurrection, but they act

Worship on Sunday by the early Christian Jews

as corroborating evidence. These facts are consistent with the idea that the Resurrection took place.

{Show a calendar with Sunday specially marked.}

Why did they meet on Sunday for worship?

{Wait for response.}

In order to celebrate the Resurrection, which they believed occurred on Sunday, these early Christian Jews chose to meet for worship on the first day of the week.

Easter

{Using the same calendar, display a circled Easter.}

This annual Christian celebration had its origin in the first centuries of the Christian church. Doesn't it make sense that it originated in the literal, physical Resurrection of Christ?

Art of the early Christians

In the first century catacombs, there is art that demonstrates a strong faith in the resurrected Lord.

One symbol is a monogram of Christ that is formed by intersecting two letters of the Greek alphabet: *X* (*chi*) and *P* (*ro*), which are the first two letters of the Greek word "Christòs" or "Christ."

The alpha and omega, the first and last letters in the Greek alphabet, were etched into this monogram to signify that Jesus is the beginning and end of all things.

Engraved into the walls of the first century catacombs was also the fish symbol, with some interesting letters etched inside. I-CH-TH-U-S {put this English transliteration on the board, with the dashes} **is actually an**

acronym for the Greek words: Iesùs Christòs Theòu Uiòs {wee-os} Soter. {Point to the letters on the board as you pronounce these words.} **These words mean: JESUS CHRIST, GOD'S SON, SAVIOR. The fish (ichthùs) is a symbol of the Christian church.** {Draw Christian fish symbol on the board with Greek letters (or transliteration) inside.} **You can see how highly the early Christians esteemed Jesus."**

Resurrection is consistent with the [life] of Jesus.

The Resurrection bonds remarkably well with all of Jesus' life.

The Resurrection is what we should expect of Him, considering His predictions, His claims, His miracles[2] and His character—all that Christ was, said, or did.

Gospel Creed of 1 Cor. 15 dates very [early].

{Briefly display 1 Cor. 15:1–8 on an overhead projector or as a digital slide (See Supplemental section). Label it "The Gospel Creed." Have students read it in unison (appoint someone the leader).}

The first few verses of 1 Cor. 15 are a [creed] that was given to Paul in the mid-[thirties], just a few years after the Resurrection. This creed presents the basic facts of the death and resurrection of Christ, with a list of people who saw Him resurrected.

{Draw a timeline showing the date of Crucifixion, the date Paul probably received the creed, and the date of the writing of 1 Corinthians.}

If you want to know what the first Christians in the early thirties believed actually happened, read this creed.

What is the significance of this early creed?

{Wait for response.}

5 years 20 years
Paul receives creed
Paul writes 1 Cor. 15
AD 30 AD 35 AD 55

It is hard to overemphasize the importance of these verses in 1 Corinthians. The evidence of this early creed[3] destroys the myth or legend theories, since with it we are, for all practical purposes, back to the original events.

Unique exaltation of Jesus after the resurrection.

Immediately after the Resurrection, Jesus was [worshiped] as Lord of Life.

We know from Roman history, the N.T. documents and the early church fathers that the first-century Christians worshiped Christ. How can we explain that apart from the Resurrection? Why would any monotheistic group worship a dead man?

Existence of the Christian Church

Percentage of Christians—World Population

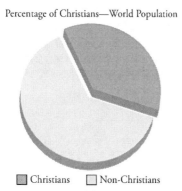

Christians ▢ Non-Christians

{Show a chart of the world population, with Christians being 1/3 of the chart. (See supplemental section). Of course, not all of the people that call themselves Christians are Christian in the biblical sense.}

Does anyone know the population of the world? {Wait for response. About 6 billion.} What percent of the world call themselves Christians? {Wait for response.} Almost 1/3 of the 6 billion—almost two billion people—call themselves Christians. How did these people come to be? Of course, just being big doesn't mean you have a legitimate beginning. And, not all of these people are true Christians. But the Resurrection is an adequate explanation for rapid growth and spread of Christianity. Christianity did not grow by force, as the Communists or Islam did, but by another impetus, the literal resurrection of a dead man.

{Write WE ARGUE on board and have the students read and recite the outline until they don't need to glance at their notes for successful recitation.}

THE LAWS OF THE LEARNER APPLIED:

Using the acrostic WE ARGUE will help the students master these arguments for the resurrection by making the material *Mindeasy.* Having the students read and recite the outline until they have it learned is the *Memorize* step of the Retention Method.

IV. What Does the Resurrection Prove?

That Jesus is who He [claimed] to be—the Son of God, God in the flesh.

Only God has the power to raise the dead, and God would not raise a liar. We will later show that He did make the claim to be God.

It also confirms the [Atonement].

It gives validity to Jesus' claim that His death would "ransom many."

It shows that He can overcome [death].

It suggests that He is able to give life to His followers, as He promised.

{For the rest of the class period, prepare for a "trial" that will occur next time you meet. The students involved will want to spend some time preparing. This activity will take almost the entire session next time. The defendant will be someone who is teaching the Resurrection as a historical fact in a public school. The prosecution says that the defendant should not teach the Resurrection because it is not a historical fact. The Prosecuting Attorney will give reasons why the Resurrection did not take place. He will have two witnesses that help him, largely by trying to point out discrepancies in John and Mark's account (you could use the example from Lesson 8). The Defense Attorney makes a case for the defendant, arguing that since the Resurrection of Jesus did take place historically, the defendant has the right to teach it. He cross-examines the prosecution's witnesses. He brings his own witnesses forward, maybe including a "medical expert." The witnesses help the defense attorney present the evidence for the Resurrection, mainly evidence contained in notes—HEART and WE ARGUE. The rest of the class can be the jury. The judge (you) will read the decision of the jury.}

V. Application of Lesson

Prepare for the trial next session.

Share the HEART and WE ARGUE acrostics with someone.

NOTES

[1] Lee Strobel, *The Case for Christ*, Zondervan, Grand Rapids, p. 195, 1998.

[2] Some students may ask you about those who have a problem with the Resurrection because it is a miracle, one of many that Jesus performed. The skeptics say, 'You can't prove a miracle." But the miracle of the Resurrection was of such a nature that it could be substantiated in court. It wasn't, for instance, a psychosomatic healing. Even though the Resurrection would be a very unusual event, the evidence for it could be taken to court, where a case could be made. Eyewitnesses could say, "I saw Jesus alive before He was crucified." Others could say, "I saw this same man nailed to a cross. I saw Him die." Others could say, "I saw this same man alive after the crucifixion." If a person is alive, dead, and alive again, he has been resurrected. This miracle is the kind of miracle that can be proven in court beyond a reasonable doubt.

[3] "That this material is traditional and pre-Pauline is evident from the technical terms delivered and received, the parallelism and somewhat stylized content, the proper names of Cephas and James, the non-Pauline words, and the possibility of an Aramaic original." (J. Sire, *Why should I Believe Anything At All?* InterVarsity Press, Downers Grove, IL, p. 157, 1995). Paul probably received the creed when he first met with Peter and James.

𝓼𝟢 FULFILLED PROPHECY

{To start the lesson, set up an impromptu Panel. Seat 3 "futurists" at the front of the class and ask them the following questions:

First set of questions: What will the weather be like tomorrow? Who will be the next president? Will things get better or worse in the next 20 years?

(Clearly distinguish the first set from the second set.)

Second set of questions: Who will be elected president in 2080? Where will he be born? What city and state? What unusual things will accompany his life? What unique gifts will he have? What unique titles will he possess? Will he die in an unusual manner? If so, how will he die? In what year will he die?}

What percentage of the panel's first set of predictions do you think will actually come true? What percentage of their second set of predictions do you think will actually come true? The first set of questions I asked them were either very general or close enough in time for them to be answered with an educated guess. The second set of questions belong to another category. How in the world could anyone predict things so specific several decades in advance? The Bible prophecies concerning the Messiah belong to this second category. It is amazing

---

THE LAWS OF THE LEARNER APPLIED:

The panel discussion will build the need for the arguments for Jesus' deity that are based on Messianic prophecy.

that prophets predicted specific unmistakable events hundreds of years in advance, and these predictions literally came to pass. We are going to show today how the fulfillment of Messianic prophecies validates the claims of Jesus.

{Read through the list of prophecies before looking up any fulfillment Scriptures. Then look up a few Scriptures according to the time you have.}

I. What Prophecies Did the Messiah Have to Fulfill?

He had to fulfill about five dozen prophecies. Here are 13 of them. These prophecies were considered to be Messianic by the Jewish Rabbis who lived before Jesus. I am not presenting them in chronological order of fulfillment. They are in a particular order so you can remember them. We are going to use the acronym THE BIBLE TALKS. The Bible talks very plainly and specifically about the future:

Prophecy	Fulfillment
Tribe of Judah Genesis 49:10	Luke 3:23, 33
House of David Jeremiah 23:5	Luke 3:23, 31
Enter Jerusalem on a [donkey] Zechariah 9:9	Matt. 21:1–8

Prophecy	Fulfillment
Born at [Bethlehem] Micah 5:2	Matt 2:1
Introduced by a messenger Isaiah 40:3	Matt. 3:1–3
Body [pierced] in crucifixion Zechariah 12:10	John 19:34
Laid to rest with the rich Isaiah 53:9	Matt. 27:57–60
Endure wounds and bruises Isaiah 53:5	Matt. 27:26
Teaching and healing ministry Isaiah 61:1, 2; 32:3–4; 35:5	Matt. 9:35; Luke 4:17–21
Arrive before the Temple and Jerusalem destroyed Daniel 9:26	Temple, Jerusalem destroyed AD 70
Labeled Lord and [God] Jeremiah 23:6, Isaiah 9:6	John 20:28; Luke 2:11
Killed 483 years after decree to rebuild Jerusalem Daniel 9:25–26	Gospels, history (Christ died about AD 30)
Silent before accusers Isaiah 53:7	Matt. 27:12

{You may want to spend time with the prophecy that Jesus would be killed 483 years after the decree to rebuild Jerusalem.[1] Ask the class after you move through the list filling in the blanks, but before you look up any passages of fulfillment: "Do you know of anybody who belonged to the tribe of Judah and to the house of David, entered Jerusalem on a donkey, was born at Bethlehem, was introduced by a messenger... ?" Go through the whole list very rapidly. It will be best if you do this with the first six, and then do it again with all of them when you get to the end. This will make the point that there were several very specific prophecies that needed to be fulfilled, and Jesus was the only one to fulfill them.}

{Remember the prophecies with the acrostic THE BIBLE TALKS. (Have this sentence written on the board in all caps.) The Bible talks very plainly and specifically about future events. Review the list at least three times.}

{Have students see if they can, using THE BIBLE TALKS for a memory aid, recite the 13 prophecies more quickly than you. Appoint a timekeeper. Present the prophecies, then have a pair of students challenge you (they can help each other). If one student wants to challenge you by himself, that may be even better. After the challenge, present the prophecies again. After this, have someone else (or another pair) challenge you. And so on.}

THE LAWS OF THE LEARNER APPLIED:

The acrostic THE BIBLE TALKS was put together to make the material "mind-easy." Through reviewing the list, the students will *Memorize* the prophecies.

II. What Is the Probability that Jesus Fulfilled Those Prophecies by Chance?

We have only listed 13 of several dozen prophecies fulfilled by Jesus. A very conservative estimate of the probability of these 13 prophecies being fulfilled by chance is 1 in 100,000,000,000,000,000. (1 in 100 quintillion); 1 in 10^{17} (one in 10 to the seventeenth power). {Write out the numbers on the board.} **This is the same probability as if we covered the entire state of Texas with silver dollars two feet deep, marked one with a red "X"...** {Use your body (gestures, etc.) to help the students visualize the scenario.} **... sent in a blindfolded man and told him to pick up one coin whenever he wished, and he picked the one with the red "X." His chances would be 1 in 10^{17}, or 1 in 100 quintillion.**[2]

If these prophecies were not fulfilled by chance, then how could they be fulfilled? Most of them could not be deliberately fulfilled. The predictions must have come from someone who could look into the future.[3] Since only God knows the future, these predictions must have come from God. And whoever fulfills them must be the one that God preordained to fulfill them.

{The teacher should play the role of a Jew who does not believe that Jesus is Messiah. Have a student come up to prove to you from memory that Jesus fulfilled Messianic prophecy and therefore qualifies. He will present the list of prophecies and claim that Jesus fulfilled them. You object by saying that Jesus fulfilled those prophecies by chance. (Don't let him/her present the illustration until you object.) He counters by sharing the probability of that happening by chance, using the Texas illustration.}

III. What Do These Fulfilled Prophecies Demonstrate?

They demonstrate that Jesus was the predicted [Messiah], and since the Messiah was to be divine, it shows that Jesus was [God].

The fact that at least a dozen detailed prophecies concerning the Messiah were fulfilled hundreds of years after the predictions demonstrates that the prophecies came from an all-knowing divine being who orchestrated the coming of Jesus, and intended for Him to be considered the Jewish Messiah!

IV. Application of Lesson

A. This week, discuss the fulfillment of Messianic prophecies with an unbeliever. Present the list of prophecies that Jesus fulfilled hundreds of years after the predictions. Use the Texas illustration to show the improbability that these prophecies were fulfilled by chance. In the space below, record his/her reactions.

B. Share the following illustration with the same unbeliever:

A prognosticator predicted 50 things about you. They all came true except one. The last one was conditional: If you drive down a certain street on a certain day, you will die in a fiery car crash. Would you drive down that street? In light of the fact that Jesus fulfilled at least 49 prophecies of the Bible (they all came true), are you going to ignore one more prophecy that says that if you don't receive Jesus, you will be separated from God forever? In the space below, describe what happened when you presented this.

> **THE LAWS OF THE LEARNER APPLIED:**
>
> The assignment is the *Master* step in the Retention Method. Through using the material on prophecy, the students will begin to "master the minimum."

NOTES

[1] The students will be very interested in this very specific prophecy. Whoever was going to be Messiah had to live and die about the same time that Jesus of Nazareth lived and died. The decree to rebuild Jerusalem was given around 445 BC. Daniel said that there would be 69 weeks (of years) between that decree and the death of the Messiah (He would be cut off). This means that there would be 483 prophetic years (One prophetic year=360 days) between the decree and the death of the Messiah. If you multiply 483 by 360, divide by 365.25, then subtract the amount from 445 (BC), you will determine that the death of the Messiah would occur around AD 31. (We don't necessarily know the exact dates of the decree or the crucifixion, but we do know the "ballpark" numbers.) It is amazing that the crucifixion of a certain man called Jesus Christ, who had fulfilled several other Messianic prophecies, occurred around that very time. You will want to draw a timeline for these dates if you present this to your students. For further information, look in *The Case for Jesus the Messiah*, by John Ankerberg.

[2] Illustration from Peter Stoner in his book *Science Speaks*. Stoner and the classes he taught determined the probabilities of eight particular Messianic prophecies being fulfilled. The probability of each prophecy coming true by chance was calculated, then all the probabilities were multiplied together. The probabilities were estimated very conservatively. In this lesson we are taking 13 prophecies, some of them different than the ones that Stoner looked at, and estimating conservatively that the probability is the same as Stoner's calculation for eight prophecies.

[3] Critics have no basis for their assertion that the prophecies were made "after the fact." It is easy to demonstrate that these prophecies were made at least 200 years before the time of Christ. How? The Septuagint (the Greek translation of the Hebrew O.T.) was written by about that time. Of course, if the O.T. prophecies were translated from Hebrew to Greek by AD 200, they must have been written earlier. The Dead Sea Scrolls also show that many of the prophecies had to be written at least 100 years before Christ. For example, the Isaiah Scroll (St. Mark's Manuscript) is dated by scholars at 100 BC. Many of the Messianic prophecies are in Isaiah. Other evidence, biblical and otherwise, shows that the prophecies were written at least 400–1,000 years before Christ. As far as reliability goes, both the Septuagint and the Dead Sea Scrolls show that the O.T. prophecies that we have recorded in our Bibles are essentially the same as was originally written. Based on all the evidence, it is remarkable that all these prophecies, written hundreds of years before Christ, are so specifically fulfilled in Jesus.

11 THE DEITY OF CHRIST

Have you heard of the T.V. evangelist Kenneth Copeland? He is a leading teacher of the Faith Movement. According to Copeland, Christ came to him in a vision and told him:

"Don't be disturbed when people put you down and speak harshly and roughly of you. They spoke that way of Me, should they not speak that way of you? The more you get to be like Me, the more they're going to think that way of you. They crucified Me for claiming that I was God. But I didn't claim I was God; I just claimed I walked with Him and that He was in Me. Hallelujah!"[1]

Copeland claims that Jesus told him that He did not claim to be God. Many others would agree with Copeland and would say that Jesus did not claim to be God. Is this true? Or is there good evidence that Jesus did claim to be divine?

How would you respond to this letter?

{Put a transparency on the overhead or display a digital slide (see Supplemental section) showing a letter that objects to the idea that Jesus claimed to be God. Read it; then give students two minutes to try to write a letter back in response. After they have spent a couple minutes on it, tell them that they will work on this letter more at the end of the lesson. Tell them that this lesson will help them to know what to write. Wait until this activity is finished before you have them open their student notes.}

If Jesus did claim to be God, He was the [only] leader of a major world religion to do so.

For example, Mohammed never claimed to be God; Buddha never claimed to be God. If it is true that Jesus claimed to be God, this would set Christ and Christianity apart from any other major religion. He would be unique. It is a gigantic thing for someone to claim to be the transcendent Creator God.

We are going to look at Christ's claims during His ministry and His claims during His trial.

I. Christ's Claims during His Ministry

A. He claimed to be the I AM of the Old Testament.

John 8:58: "Before Abraham was, [I AM]."

This is an identity with the great "I AM" of Exodus 3:14. Remember Moses at the burning bush? When he asked God, "Who shall I say sent me to the Israelites," God said, "Say that I AM has sent you." For Jesus to claim he was I AM was to claim he was Jehovah.

John 8:24: "If you do not believe that [I AM], you shall die in your sins."

The "he" that comes after I AM in this verse (in your Bible) is not in the Greek text. Not

only is Jesus claiming deity, He is also saying that we must believe that He is deity in order to be saved.

Jesus not only referred to Himself as the I AM of the Old Testament, but also…

B. He claimed to be One with God the Father.

Declaration by Jesus: "I and My Father are [One]."

Response of the Jews: Took up stones to stone Him.

Why? "You, being a [man], make yourself to be [God]" (John 10:30).

Clearly, the Jews understood that He was claiming to be God.

What would you think of me if I were to stand before you and tell you that "Before Abraham was, I Am"?

{At this point, talk and act like you think you are God. Stand on a chair. Talk in an "important" voice.}

You know—unless you believe that I Am, you will die in your sins. I and God the Father are one! If you believe in me, you will have eternal life! I am the way. I am the truth. No one can go to Heaven unless they come through me! {Pause.}

How many of you believe in me? {Pause.} Do you understand the kinds of claims Jesus was making? If Jesus wasn't God, He was an egomaniac, at the very least. One thing you will notice if you study the sayings of Jesus—He placed Himself above His teachings. For example, He said, "I am the way," not "I will show you the way."

{During the next section, have students read the Scripture verses that you had asked them to look up. Have all the students write the references into their notes.}

THE LAWS OF THE LEARNER APPLIED:

The teacher is building the need with his voice and his actions when he pretends that he believes he is God. He is also reviewing the material in accordance with the Law of Retention.

C. Christ claimed to POSSESS DIVINE ATTRIBUTES.

1. OMNIPRESENCE

{Have student read Matt. 18:20—"Where two or three are gathered... "}

2. ETERNITY

{Have student read John 17:5, 24—"the glory I had with thee before the world was."}

D. Christ claimed POWER TO PERFORM DIVINE ACTS.

1. To [forgive] sins

Look at Mark 2. After Jesus claimed to forgive the paralytic, the Jews criticized Him, saying among themselves, "Only God can forgive sins." Jesus, knowing their thoughts, did something to prove that He had the divine power to forgive, as God. What did He do? He healed the paralytic.

He healed as God to prove He had the power to forgive as God.

2. To [resurrect] those who believe in Him

{Have student read John 6:40.}

3. To give [eternal life]

{Have students read John 4:14 and John 10:27–28.}

{Drill the four major claims and their sub-points; have all the students read or recite them together twice.}

{Call a student up to the front of class. Have him be the "non-Christian." Sit down with him and briefly summarize (90 seconds) the claims that Christ made, proving to your "non-Christian" student that Jesus did claim to be God. Then have another student who was watching play your role in front of class, proving to yet another student that Jesus claimed to be God. After this, praise the student and tell him how he could have done better.}

THE LAWS OF THE LEARNER APPLIED:

With the earlier presentation, the teacher *Instructed*. When he sat down with a student to discuss whether Jesus claimed to be God, he *Illustrated* the skill of using this information in informal conversation. Having another student prove to someone else the same concept, the teacher *Improved* the student.

II. Christ's Claims at the Trial

A. The Question: Mark 14:61—"Are you the Christ, the Son of the Blessed?"

B. The Answer: Mark 14:62—"I am."

1. Jesus claims to be the [MESSIAH].

Was Jesus claiming divinity by claiming to be the Messiah? Was the predicted Messiah supposed to be God? Yes, according to Isaiah 9:6 and Jeremiah 23:6. Jeremiah 23:6 says that the Messiah's name will be "The LORD (*Yahweh*) our Righteousness." Isaiah 9:6 says that the Messiah will be called "Mighty God."[2]

2. Jesus claims to be the [SON OF GOD].

Was Jesus claiming to be a son of God in the sense that we are all sons of God? No. Jesus claimed to be the only Son of God. Earlier He had said, "For God so loved the world that He gave His only-begotten Son"(John 3:16). For Him to be the Son of God meant that He had a one-of-a-kind relationship with the Father. Jesus claimed that He, the only Son, was pre-existent—since He was sent into the world by the Father (John 3:16). Jesus also said that He dwelt in the bosom of the Father (John 1:18). This was a very special Father-Son relationship. Remember John 10:30? Jesus said that He and the Father were one. In fact, Jesus said that we must honor the Son as we do the Father (John 5:23). For Jesus to claim to be the Son of God meant that He was claiming to be one in essence with God the Father. You can see why the Jewish leaders were upset at Christ's affirmation that He was the Son of God.

3. Jesus claims to be the [SON OF MAN].

In response to the question at the trial, Jesus said, "You will see the Son of Man sitting at the right hand of the Power, and coming with the clouds of heaven." This was a reference to:

Daniel 7:13-14: "I was watching in the night visions, and behold, One like the Son of Man, coming with the clouds of heaven!"

The term "Son of Man" is a Messianic title.

C. The Conviction: Jesus was not convicted for what He did or said He did. He was convicted for who He said He [was].

{Review. Have students explain how the claim to be the Messiah was a claim to deity. Have them also explain the significance of Jesus claiming to be the Son of God. The answers are in the notes above.}

So, did Jesus claim to be God? {Wait for response.} **Yes He did!**

III. Conclusion: Jesus claimed to be [God].

The fact that He fulfilled prophecies and that He arose from the dead proved that He was who He said He was—God come in the flesh.

{Have students finish responding to the letter by someone who doesn't believe that Jesus claimed to be God. Give them 3 more minutes to work on this activity, using their notes. When the time is up, have a couple students read what they have written (even though they may not have finished). Offer critique and encourage the students to keep sharing this information.}

{Have students practice putting the blocks together, now that the argument has reached the third premise.}

IV. Application of Lesson

Finish writing your letter, explaining to someone why you believe that Jesus claimed to be God. Use appropriate Scripture verses.

NOTES

[1] Kenneth Copeland, quoted by Hank Hanegraaff, *Christianity in Crisis*, Harvest House, Eugene, OR, p. 137–138, 1993.
[2] If the students want more evidence, have them look up Psalm 110:1: "The LORD said to my Lord. . ."

12 THE CLOSING ARGUMENTS

{Ask students if they finished writing their letters about the claims of Christ. Have a student read what he wrote. Comment on the letter.}

{Get five students to help you with the following reading, beginning on the next page. You will need to make five copies of the reading. You be the narrator. Have your students come to the front. Present the scenario after you have assigned the roles, which are listed below.}

{Chairman,

Narrator,

Toe-scum,

Objector,

Spew-bile,

Another demon.}

THE GOOD TEACHER MYTH

Chairman: "Devils and Underdevils come to order!"

Narrator: An unholy convocation of fallen angels commenced in the cavernous meeting room of Underearth.

Chairman: "This session has been ordered by the Evil One himself to discuss and decide strategy that will prevent humans from returning to the Enemy. A suggestion has been offered by Toe-scum."

Narrator: A hideous, wart-faced devil rose from the front row and turned to face the devilish assembly.

Toe-scum: "My despised colleagues,"

Narrator: Toe-scum began,

Toe-scum: "I propose that our darkstars assigned to the world's cults and 'isms' and organized religions put forth the idea that the Enemy's Son was a 'good teacher.'"

Objector: "Curse you, Toe-Scum!"

Narrator: Spewed an objector who had risen to his horny feet on Toe-scum's right.

Objector: "You should be cannibalized by the Assembly for suggesting friendly treatment of the Enemy's Son!"

Narrator: Several demons around Toe-scum licked their crusted lips in anticipation.

Toe-scum: "You imbecile,"

Narrator: Toe-scum retorted.

Toe-scum: "This is no friendly treatment I propose."

Narrator: He straightened proudly.

Toe-scum: "My suggestion is truly diabolical."

Narrator: Another devil stood.

Another demon: "How can you call such a simple-minded idea 'diabolical'?"

Toe-scum: "Because,"

Narrator: He replied,

Toe-scum: "To label Him a 'good teacher' will effectively class Him with Moses, Zoroaster, Mohammed … it is to damn Him with faint praise."

Narrator: A silence of realization descended on the crowd.

Toe-scum:	"Don't you see, you half-wits, if humans believe He is only a 'good teacher,' they can dismiss His Lordship, His Divinity?"
Spew-bile:	"No,"
Narrator:	Responded a devil called Spew-bile.
Spew-bile:	"They'll never fall for that! He Himself made it very clear who He is."
Objector:	"Spew-bile's right,"
Narrator:	Said the original objector to the idea.
Spew-bile:	"Humans have The Book. They know that He said Himself, 'Before Abraham was, I AM.' They've read His words about the glory He shared with the Father before the world began." "Yes, you fool,"
Narrator:	Spew-bile added.
Spew-bile:	"They know He claimed the power to read men's minds and hearts and to forgive sins. They have His words, 'I have come down from heaven.' They know that He claimed to have power to raise Himself from the dead and that witnesses confirmed His Resurrection. They're not so foolish as to think a mere man, a 'good teacher' could do those things! And,"
Narrator:	Asserted Spew-bile with finality,
Spew-bile:	"They will recognize that if those things He claimed about Himself were not true, then He was not a 'good teacher' … He was a liar or a lunatic!"
Narrator:	A murmur arose in the room. Some demons around Toe-scum again licked their lips and looked at him with hungry eyes, but he appeared confident.
Toe-scum:	"I must remind my contemptible comrades of the human tendency that allows us such frequent success. Mortals will often choose a lie even when they know the truth. As the Enemy's Son Himself said in one of His stories, 'If they do not listen to Moses and the prophets, they will not be convinced even if someone rises from the dead.'"
Narrator:	Toe-scum's lips parted in a sneering smile as he sat down. The hungry demons surrounding him exchanged disappointed glances.
Chairman:	"Toe-scum's proposal,"
Narrator:	Bellowed the Chairman,
Chairman:	"Meets with the approval of the Demonic Council. The propagation of the 'Good Teacher Myth' is now an official strategy of Hell."[1]

This imaginary story shows how the forces of darkness have actually deceived people into rejecting Christ as Lord. Many people choose to believe that Jesus is simply a Good Teacher, but is that a reasonable option?

Here is an indisputable fact: The New Testament portrays Jesus as a man who claims to be God.

What are we to do with this? We are actually presented with a Quintilemma (five options). Look at the flowchart in your notes. Flip a couple pages to get to this chart.

{The flowchart on the next page can be shown "as is" if the class is small enough, summarized on the marker board, or displayed as a PowerPoint slide (this last option is ideal). Go through each option, explaining them. Afterward, refute the four erroneous options.}

THE QUINTILEMMA

The New Testament presents Jesus as an historical man who claims to be God.

New Testament is correct.

There was a man named Jesus who claimed to be God.

New Testament is incorrect.

There was not a man named Jesus who claimed to be God.

Jesus is a [**Legend**].

Jesus meant to be taken in a mystical sense.

We are as much God as He is. He believed that God is All, and All is God.

Jesus is a [**Guru**].

Jesus meant to be taken literally.

He taught that He was the Transcendent Creator.

The claim of deity was false.

The claim of deity was true.

Jesus is [**LORD**].

He knew it was false.

Jesus is a [**Liar**].

He didn't know it was false.

Jesus is a [**Lunatic**].

There are no other options: Jesus was either a Legend, a Guru, a Liar, a Lunatic, or Lord. Let's look at these options one by one.

I. Why Not a Legend?

Could Jesus have been a legend? Maybe He didn't exist as a person or at least didn't say or do the things the N.T. claims. Is this a reasonable option? Why not? {Wait for response.}

No, He couldn't be a legend. We have already shown that:

The N.T. is historically [reliable], confirmed by the Bibliographical Test, [Internal] Evidence, and [External] Evidence.

The N.T. therefore gives an [accurate] picture of Jesus—what He did and what He said.

II. Why Not a Guru?

Could He be a guru? An Eastern mystic? A teacher of Hindu theology? Someone who taught that we are all one with God, which is the universe itself?

{Wait for response.}

This is not a reasonable option because:

Jesus was a Jew raised in a strictly [MONOTHEISTIC] culture.

{Write "monotheistic" on the board and explain that it means "a belief in one transcendent God."}

No one would be less likely to believe himself to be divine than a Jew.

Jesus' teaching was not the teaching of an Eastern [mystic], but that of a Jewish Rabbi who believed in [one] transcendent Creator.

So we know that Jesus was a real historical person, that He was a Jew raised in a strictly monotheistic culture, and that He taught that He was that one transcendent God.

If it is true that Jesus, as a Jewish Rabbi, taught that He was God, we need to take seriously what C. S. Lewis had to say about our options:

C. S. Lewis: "I am trying here to prevent anyone saying the really foolish thing that people often say about Him: 'I'm ready to accept Jesus as a great moral teacher, but I don't accept His claim to be God.' That is the one thing we must not say. **A man who was merely a man and said the sort of things Jesus said would not be a great [moral teacher]. He would either be a [lunatic]—on the level with the man who says he is a poached egg—or else he would be the [devil of Hell]. You must make your choice. Either this man was, and is, the Son of God: or else a [madman] or something worse.** You can shut Him up for a fool; you can spit at Him and kill Him as a demon; or you can fall at His feet and call Him Lord and God. But let us not come with any patronizing nonsense about His being a great human teacher. He has not left that open to us. He did not intend to."[2]

{After reading the quote, have students read in unison (with you) the part in bold.}

Contrary to what the underworld would like us to believe, we do not have the option to believe that Jesus was simply a good, moral teacher. We have already shown that there is no evidence that He was a teacher of pantheistic theology (pantheism meaning "a belief that everyone is God"). Nor could He have been a typical Jewish Rabbi who believed in

the Jewish God and had many good, moral things to say. He could not have been simply a good, moral teacher if, as a Jewish Rabbi, He were teaching that He was the one transcendent God of the universe. As we have seen in this quotation, C.S. Lewis points out that there are only three options left. (Being a good teacher doesn't even rate as one of the five choices in our Quintilemma.) Since Jesus did intentionally teach that He was the I AM of the Old Testament, He was either a liar, a lunatic, or He was Lord.

III. Why Not a Liar?

But why is it not reasonable to believe that He was a liar?

A major reason the "Liar Theory" is unreasonable is that Jesus is universally acknowledged to be the most pure man in history.

According to Peter Kreeft, a Christian apologist, Jesus couldn't be a liar:

"1. Because he has the wrong psychological [profile]. He was [unselfish], loving, caring, compassionate, and passionate about teaching [truth] and helping others to truth. Liars lie for [selfish] reasons, like money, fame, pleasure or power. Jesus gave up all worldly goods, and life itself."

2. Because there is no conceivable [motive] for his lie. It brought him hatred, rejection, misunderstanding, persecution, torture and [death]."[3]

Another reason to reject the idea that Jesus lied is the Resurrection. If we accept the Bible as historically reliable, we must accept Christ's Resurrection as true. Only God can raise the dead, and God would not have raised Jesus from the dead if He were a liar.

IV. Why Not a Lunatic?

But maybe He was a lunatic. For someone to sincerely believe he was the Almighty Creator and be wrong would at least be awfully close to being a lunatic. Kreeft says,

"The size of the gap between what you are and what you think you are is a pretty good index of your insanity. If I believe I am the best writer in America, I am an egotistical fool, but I am not insane. If I believe I am Napoleon, I am probably near the edge. If I believe I am the archangel Gabriel, I am probably well over it. And if I believe I am God? . . . Would you send your children to Sunday school to be taught by a man who thought he was God?"

But credible psychologists will tell you that Jesus has no marks of lunacy. He is considered to be perfectly balanced in His personality.

Why Jesus could not have been a lunatic:

"1. Because the psychological profiles are opposite. The lunatic lacks the very qualities that shine in Jesus- practical [wisdom], tough love, and unpredictable [creativity].

2. No Jew could sincerely think he was [God]. No group in history was less likely to confuse the Creator with a creature than the Jews, the only people who had an absolute, and absolutely clear, [distinction] between the divine and the human."[4]

V. What Is the Only Reasonable Option?

We must conclude therefore that Jesus was not a legend, nor a guru, nor a liar, nor a lunatic, but Lord. We must worship Him as Lord and God!

Jesus is [Lord].

{Have a student present the flowchart on the board to the whole class, explaining the options and giving brief refutations of the erroneous ones. Critique. Pair students up. Have one draw the flowchart for the other, explaining the options and giving brief refutations of the erroneous ones. Give them 2 minutes to do this. When they are done, bring the blocks back out, present the general argument for Christianity with the blocks, and then go through the premises again, having the students fill out the blanks on their final page of notes.}

CONCLUSIONS

IS THE BIBLE THE WORD OF GOD AND JESUS THE ONLY WAY TO HEAVEN?

Premise A: The New Testament is historically accurate; it is a basically [reliable] and trustworthy document.

Premise B: On the basis of this reliable document, we have sufficient evidence to believe that Jesus [rose] from the dead as He predicted He would, and that He fulfilled dozens of other Messianic prophecies.

Premise C: Jesus' Resurrection and fulfillment of prophecy show that He was who He said He was: the [Messiah], the Son of God—[God] in the flesh.

Premise D: As the Son of God (God the Son), Jesus Christ is an [infallible] authority—What He says is absolutely trustworthy.

Premise E: Jesus Christ taught that the Bible is the [Word of God] (Matt 5:18, 15:4; Mark 12:36; Luke 24:44–46). He also taught that He was the only way to God (John 14:6).

{Look up these Scriptures.}

Conclusion: If Christ said it, we must believe it. The Bible is the Word of [God], and Jesus is the Only Way to God.

{Have a team of three students build the blocks again (in front of class), but this time, after they are done, have three "skeptical" students challenge them to defend the premises. For example, when they say that the prophecies and Resurrection prove that He was who He said He was, the students might say, "But I don't even think He claimed to be God." Have the "apologists" respond. Jump in to help them as necessary.}

{Commend students for their great work and encourage them to continue to master apologetic skills.}

THE LAWS OF THE LEARNER APPLIED:

The students are *Involved* and *Improved* when they attempt to build the blocks again and defend the structure against the attacks of the "skeptics."

APPLICATION OF LESSON:

A. Present the flowchart to an unbeliever who may have doubts about the deity of Christ.

B. Present the diagram of the general argument for Christianity to someone who doubts the validity of Christianity.

NOTES

[1] Josh McDowell, *Don't Check Your Brains at the Door*, W Publishing Group, Nashville, pp. 18–19, 1992.
[2] C.S. Lewis, *Mere Christianity*, HarperSanFrancisco, San Francisco, pp. 55–56, 2001.
[3] Peter Kreeft, *Handbook on Christian Apologetics*, InterVarsity Press, Downers Grove, IL, p. 160, 1994.
[4] Ibid., pp. 160–161.

Supplemental
materials

THE BASIC MESSAGE OF THE BIBLE

(A GOSPEL PRESENTATION)

Start by asking people what they think the basic message of the Bible is.

Affirm their response, then say, "May I show you a little diagram that shows what I see to be the basic message of the Bible?"

If they give you permission, say the following as you draw the diagram to the left (add figures, shapes, or words as you first mention the concepts associated with them):

The basic message of the Bible is this: **God** *made* **us**, *the human family, to have a holy* **love** *relationship with Him. But the first man* **sinned**, *and as a result, pain and death came into the world, and the rest of the human family (including you and I) were born with a selfish, sinful nature. And we have sinned ourselves. Our sin brought a great gulf between us and God. The Bible calls that separation* **death**. *In fact, if we die physically while being spiritually dead, we will forever be separated from God in a place called* **hell**. *That is the bad news of the Bible.*

The good news is that God loves us and doesn't want us to go to hell (John 3:16). So, God the Father sent God the Son, Jesus, into the world to die on the cross and rise from the dead so that we could have our relationship to God restored. In his sacrificial death, Jesus, the sinless God-man, satisfied the holy justice of God so we could be forgiven. Through his resurrection, Jesus conquered death and became the bridge back to God. Now if we **repent**—*if we turn away from all our sins (Acts 3:19)—and if we* **receive** *Christ into our hearts and lives—trusting Him to forgive us (John 1:12)—then we will in a moment of time pass from death to life (we will cross the bridge). We will enter into a relationship with God, becoming a new creation. And in the end, all those who have trusted in Christ alone for salvation will go to* **heaven** *to spend eternity in happy fellowship with God and with others who know God. That is the basic message of the Bible.*

So…could I ask you where you see yourself on this diagram? Are you on the "God" side, are you on the left side running away from all of this, or are you on the edge ready to step over?… Where do you want to be?… Is there anything stopping you from stepping over right now?

Go to www.answersingenesis.org/go/defending-your-faith for a step-by-step PowerPoint presentation of this message.

THE DISAPPEARING PENNY

MATERIALS:

- **A clear drinking glass**
- **A piece of white paper, cut to the size of the top of the drinking glass. (The audience doesn't see this covering because the top of the tumbler is placed on a white sheet of paper during the trick.)**
- **Glue, to bond the paper to the glass**
- **A regular size piece of white paper**
- **A tube made of construction paper or poster board that fits perfectly over the glass.**

THE TRICK:

The penny is placed on the white sheet of paper. The clear drinking glass is resting on the sheet, top down. The audience can see through the glass. Tell the audience that you have a special tube that will suck the penny right through the bottom of the glass.

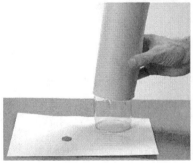

The tube is placed over the glass.

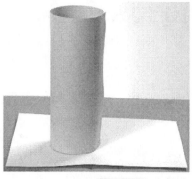

Then the glass (with the tube) is placed over the penny.

As you pull the tube away from the glass, it will look as if the penny has disappeared.

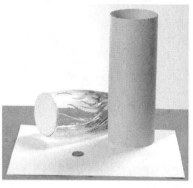

Tell the audience that the special tube has made the penny disappear. Put the tube back over the glass, move the glass, and the audience will see that you have brought the penny back. Repeat.

This trick is truly mysterious, because most people will not figure out that the top of the glass is covered with white paper, thus making the penny invisible when the glass is placed over it.

APPLICATION:

Explain the trick. Tell the audience that even though it appeared that the penny had disappeared, it really was there all the time. Believing that the penny was gone didn't make it so. It is possible to believe something that is not true. Belief is not the same as truth. Some people think that you create your own spiritual reality by believing it, but what you believe and the reality may be totally different.

THE EYE

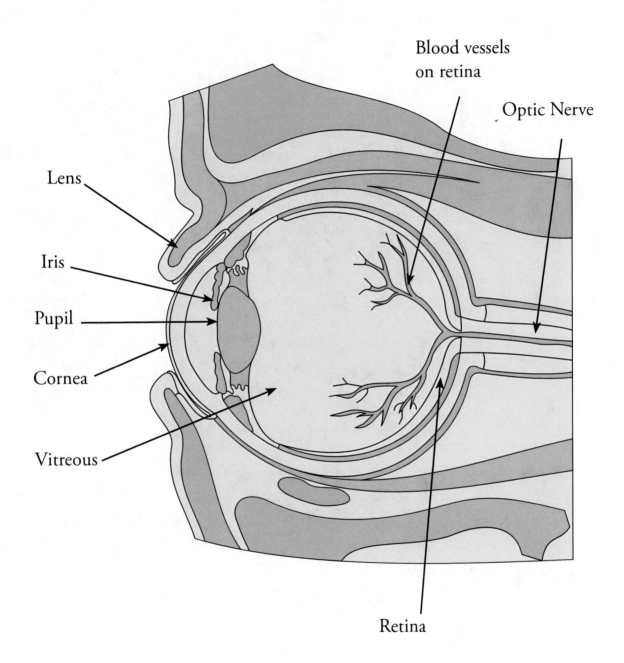

Lens

Iris

Pupil

Cornea

Vitreous

Blood vessels
on retina

Optic Nerve

Retina

THE CELL

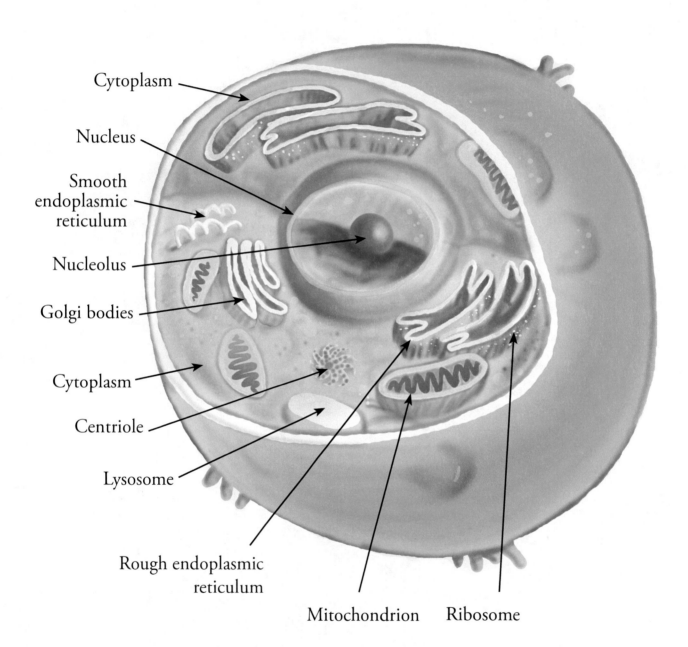

Cytoplasm

Nucleus

Smooth endoplasmic reticulum

Nucleolus

Golgi bodies

Cytoplasm

Centriole

Lysosome

Rough endoplasmic reticulum

Mitochondrion   Ribosome

DNA

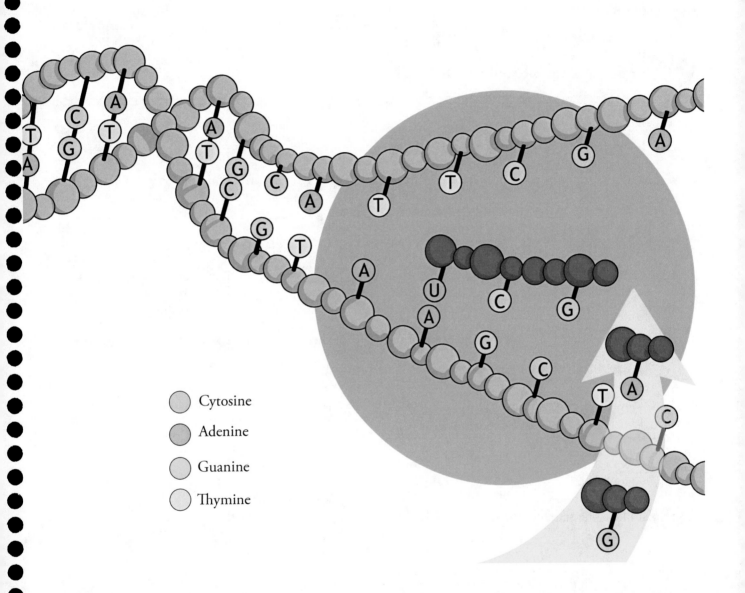

Cytosine

Adenine

Guanine

Thymine

QUIZ ONE

1. Apologetics is presenting _____ for the _____ of Christianity.

2. Apologetics helps to _____ our faith and helps us as we _____ our faith.

3. The use of apologetics is commanded in I Peter _____.

4. Write out the entire verse.

5. Christianity cannot be proven by the scientific method because the resurrection of Jesus is not a _____ _____ event. Christianity is proven using the _____-_____ method of proof.

6. Christianity cannot be proven 100% because nothing _____ be proven with 100% certainty.

7. *True* or *False*: Since Christianity cannot be proven 100%, then we cannot know whether Christianity is true.

8. Pascal said that there is _____ evidence to convince someone of Christianity if his mind is not set against it, but there is not enough evidence to bring someone into the kingdom who _____ ____ _____ _____.

9. Explain how the statement "All truth is relative" is like | The Sentence in this Box is False. |

10. Give an illustration that shows that believing something does not make it true.

Dog Varieties

Affenpinscher

Deerhound

Lundehund

Dalmatian

Lion Dog

Karelian Bearhound

Kanaan Dog

Miniature Pinscher

Chow-chow

Collie

Kelpie

Beagle

GOLDEN NUMBERS

by Carl Wieland and Russell Grigg
First published: *Creation* **16**(4):26–29,
September 1994

What on earth do rabbits, the Parthenon, mathematics, sunflowers, art, and pinecones have to do with each other? They are all interconnected in a fascinating way, giving evidence of a beautiful, not yet fully understood patterning in the world.

Italian mathematician Leonardo Fibonacci (rhymes with "Archie"), also known later as Leonardo Pisano (Leonardo of Pisa, c. 1170–1240) theorized about the rate of multiplication of breeding pairs of rabbits beginning with one pair. He reckoned that the way in which the numbers of pairs would increase followed a mathematical progression in which each number after the first two was the sum of the two preceding numbers. That is, 0, 1, 1, 2, 3, 5, 8, 13, 21, etc. (3+5=8, 5+8=13, 8+13=21, and so on). This has become known as the Fibonacci series.

If you look at the seeds in the head of a sunflower or daisy, you will see that they are arranged in two sets of spirals, one set running clockwise, the other counterclockwise. Count the number of spirals going in one direction, and the number going in the other. You will find that these are always two numbers which are next to each other in the Fibonacci series (e.g., 8 and 13). A similar arrangement is found in the construction of pine cones, snail-shell spirals, and animal horns and in the arrangement of leaf buds on a stem.[1]

Computer modelling[2] has apparently shown that the way in which a group of circles of varying sizes is most efficiently packed is in a series of spirals that have this Fibonacci patterning—but no one yet seems to know why.[3]

PLEASING TO ARTISTS

The so-called Golden Section (or Golden Ratio), known to most artists and architects, is also related to Fibonacci patterns. If asked to choose the rectangle most pleasing to the eye from a series of rectangles, most people would choose one in which the ratio of the two sides (that is, the larger side divided by the smaller) is approximately 1.62.[4] In other words, the long side is 1.62 times the length of the shorter. A rectangle framing the front of the famous ancient Greek building, the Parthenon (below), has sides which follow this Golden Ratio. This proportion is widely found in art and architecture.

Statistical experiments have shown that "people involuntarily give preference to proportions that approximate to the Golden Section."[5] This Golden Ratio (1.62 or 1.618 to four significant figures) seems to be naturally pleasing to the human eye. Authoritative works on art and architecture make bold claims in alleging, for example, that "the Golden Section is aesthetically superior to all other proportions," which claim is said to be "supported by an immense quantity of data, collected from both nature and the arts … ."[6]

When we take the Fibonacci series (ignoring the zero), dividing each number by the one before it gives: 1, 2, 1.5, 1.6, 1.625, 1.615, 1.619, 1.617, 1.619, 1.617, 1.618, and so on, *ad infinitum*. After the first few, the numbers keep hovering around 1.618. To three significant figures, they stay precisely on this Golden Ratio of 1.62 indefinitely. No one yet seems to know why dividing these Fibonacci numbers should give proportions which happen to be pleasing to the eye.

Returning to living things, we also see that when you count the spirals on a sunflower hub one way, then the other way, dividing the larger number by the smaller gives this same Golden Ratio.

UNEXPLAINED LINK-UPS

Why should there be all these fascinating and unexplained linkups between things which are mathematically beautiful and things which are beautiful to the human eye? And why do these in turn link up to number patterns found in living things?

When interviewed on television in relation to some of these matters, a mathematician said, "I personally believe there is some greater deity that's organized it. Everything is too cleverly organized, as far as I'm personally concerned, to have just happened by happenchance. Whether you say all this was constructed by God, or whether you believe in some other way of doing it, I'm not quite sure, but yes, I think there is some power behind it all, but what it is I have no idea."[7]

Unfortunately, our young people are being indoctrinated in humanist/evolutionary fallacies which try to deny the logical conclusion of intelligent design. For example, it is commonly claimed that nature (chance) invented man's mind, which invented mathematics.[8] How then is it that we find the same mathematical patterns in nature as in that which appeals to our sense of beauty?

Surely it is more logical to conclude that the connections exist because nature, mathematics and the human mind, with its subtle sense of beauty, have one supreme link—they are all the created products of God, the Master Designer.

REFERENCES

[1] *Encyclopædia Britannica* **7**:279, 1992. Apparently, Fibonacci numbers also feature in the genealogy of descent of the male bee, but no details are provided.

[2] This was stated without detail on a *Quantum* television program, screened by Australian Broadcasting Commission, November 13, 1991.

[3] *New Scientist*, p. 18, April 18, 1992. Also *Physical Review Letters* **68**:2098. French physicists have built a physical model which seems to show that such "Fibonacci spiralling" is a result of the system's keeping the energy required for the growth of its parts (e.g., the seeds) to a minimum.

[4] Dividing any line (AB) by a point (C) such that AB/AC = AC/BC will ensure that these fractions equal the golden ratio, no matter how long the line.

[5] *The Oxford Companion to Art*, Ed. Harold Osborne, First Edition, Oxford University Press, Oxford, p.489, 1978.

[6] *Ibid.* p. 488. This claim could still be so, even if it should be claimed that the Parthenon proportions mentioned were deliberately chosen because of Greek fascination for numbers and geometry. Leonardo da Vinci was fascinated by this Golden Section, or "divine proportion" as it was also called, particularly in relation to the proportions of the human body. See also "The Geometry of Art and Life" by Matila Ghyka, and "The Divine Proportion" by H.E. Huntley, both available in Dover editions.

[7] The speaker was Dr. Michael Gore of the National Science and Technology Centre, Canberra, Australia (Ref. 2).

[8] See James Nickel, Why Does Mathematics Work?, *TJ*, vol. 4, pp. 147–157, 1990.

AUTHOR & TIME SPAN

Author/Work	Time Span
Aristotle	1,400 yrs.
Tacitus	1,000 yrs.
Caesar	950 yrs.
Odyssey	500 yrs.
New Testament	90 yrs.

AUTHOR & COPIES

Author/Work	# of Copies
Plato	7
Caesar	10
Tacitus	20
Homer	643
New Testament	5,700 (Greek)

MODEL OF HERODIAN JERUSALEM

Photo by Ken Ham

Do We Have the Original N.T.?

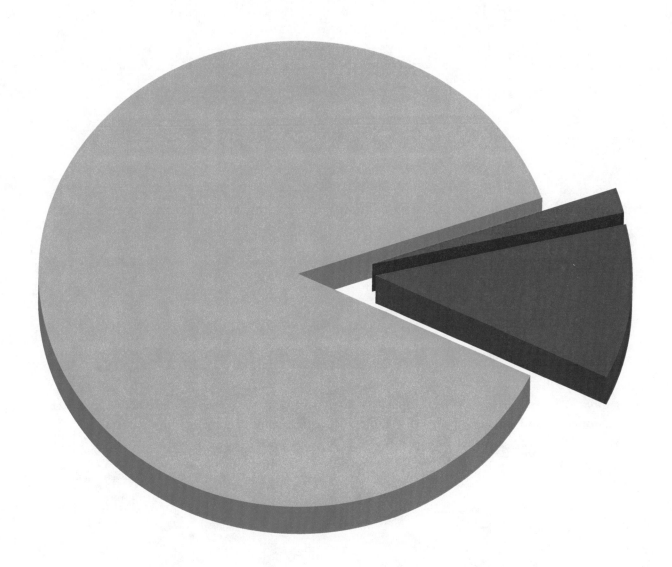

☐ No change
☐ Spelling & grammar changes
☐ Significant changes

Quiz Two

1. What are three tests that are used to determine the historical reliability of ancient documents?

2. What are the three aspects of the bibliographical test?

Refute the following objections, using as many facts, dates, and diagrams as possible:

3. *Objection:* The N.T. was written 100–200 years after the life of Christ. How do we know we don't have a distorted picture of His life due to this gap?

4. *Objection:* We do not have what was originally written because there is *too much time* between the original manuscripts and the earliest surviving copies. More time = more copying = more mistakes, and we don't even know what mistakes were made.

5. *Objection:* Even if there is a short time between the originals and the first copies, there are still *too many differences* among the surviving N.T. manuscripts for us to know what was in the original. All the copying over the years resulted in a huge number of conflicting manuscripts!

Correspondence between Pliny & the Emperor

While Pliny the Younger was governor of Bithynia in Asia Minor he wrote to the emperor Trajan concerning the Christians of his province. This was around A.D. 112. The emperor Trajan responded to Pliny's letter. These non-Christians give excellent information about early Christianity. In this dramatic presentation of the correspondence between these two men, _____ will be Pliny and _____ will be the emperor Trajan.

PLINY:

Dear Emperor,

The method I have observed toward those who have been denounced to me as Christians is this: I interrogated them whether they were in fact Christians; if they confessed it, I repeated the question twice, adding the threat of capital punishment; if they still persevered, I ordered them to be executed. For whatever the nature of their beliefs might be, I could at least feel no doubt that inflexible obstinacy deserved chastisement. There were others also possessed with the same infatuation, but being citizens of Rome, I directed them to be taken to Rome for trial.

These accusations spread (as is usually the case) from the mere fact of the matter being investigated, and several forms of the mischief came to light. A billboard was put up, without any signature, accusing a large number of persons by name. I thought it proper to discharge those who denied they were, or had ever been, Christians, and who repeated after me an invocation to the gods, and offered formal worship with frankincense before your statue, which I had ordered to be brought into Court for that purpose, and who finally cursed Christ. It is said that those who are really Christians cannot be forced into performing these acts. Others who were named by the anonymous informer at first confessed themselves Christians, and then denied it; true, they said, they had been of that persuasion but they had quitted it, some three years, others many years, and a few as much as twenty-five years previously. They all worshiped your statue and the images of the gods, and cursed Christ.

They affirmed, however, that the whole of their guilt, or their error, was that they were in the habit of meeting on a certain fixed day before it was light, when they sang in alternate verses a hymn to Christ, as to a god, and bound themselves by a solemn oath, not to perform any wicked deed, never to commit any fraud, theft or adultery, never to falsify their word, not deny a trust when they should be called upon to make it good; after which it was their custom to separate, and then reassemble to partake of food—but food of an ordinary and innocent kind. Even this practice, however, they had abandoned after the publication of my edict, by which according to your orders, I had forbidden political organization. I therefore judged it so much the more necessary to extract the real truth, with the assistance of torture, from two female slaves, who were styled deaconesses: but I could discover nothing more than depraved and excessive superstition."

Emperor Trajan:

"My dear Pliny: You have acted with perfect correctness in deciding the cases of those who have been charged before you with being Christians. Indeed, no general decision can be made by which a set form of dealing with them could be established. They must not be ferreted out; if they are charged and convicted, they must be punished, provided that anyone who denies that he is a Christian and gives practical proof of that by invoking our gods is to be pardoned on the strength of this repudiation, no matter what grounds for suspicion may have existed against him in the past. Anonymous documents which are laid before you should receive no attention in any case; they form a very bad precedent and are quite unworthy of the age in which we live."

POOL OF BETHESDA

Photo by Kevin Moser

PERCENTAGE OF CHRISTIANS WORLD POPULATION

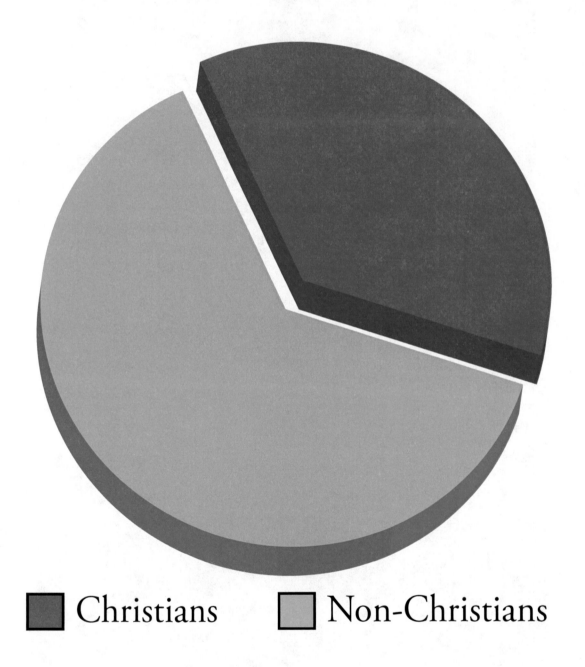

■ Christians ■ Non-Christians

THE GOSPEL CREED

For what I received I passed on to you as of first importance: that Christ died for our sin according to the Scriptures, that He was buried, that He was raised on the third day according to the Scriptures, and that He appeared to Peter and then to the twelve. After that, He appeared to more than five hundred of the brothers at the same time, most of whom are still living, though some have fallen asleep. Then He appeared to James, then to all the Apostles, and last of all he appeared to me also, as to one abnormally born.

St. Paul (I Cor. 15:3–8)

QUIZ THREE

1. Write out the HEART argument for the Resurrection.

2. Write out the WE ARGUE acrostic.

3. What does the Resurrection prove?

Skeptic's Letter

Dear Christian,

Thanks for your last letter. I want to continue to talk about the issues you have brought up.

I respect you and your beliefs, but I cannot understand why you persist in your assertion that Jesus claimed to be God. I have read through most of the gospels, and I do not remember Jesus ever standing up to declare: "I am God!" I am confident that later followers of Jesus exalted him far above what he would have wanted them to. Let's not put words in Jesus' mouth. Jesus did not claim to be God; he only said that he was *in* God.

Your friend,
Dubious

RECOMMENDED READING

The resources marked by asterisks (*) have been especially helpful in the development of this course.

Ankerberg, John and John Weldon, *Ready With An Answer*, Harvest House Publishers, Eugene, Oregon, 1997.

*Ankerberg, John, Dr. John Weldon, and Dr. Walter C. Kaiser, Jr., *The Case for Jesus the Messiah: Incredible Prophecies That Prove God Exists*, The John Ankerberg Evangelistic Association, Chattanooga, Tennessee, 1989.

Barnett, Paul, *Is the New Testament History?* Servant Books, Ann Arbor, Michigan, 1986.

Boa, Kenneth and Moody, Larry, *I'm Glad You Asked*, Victor Books, Wheaton, Illinois, 1982.

Boyd, Dr. Gregory A. and Edward K. Boyd, *Letters From A Skeptic*, Victor Books, Wheaton, Illinois 1994.

Bruce, F. F., *The New Testament Documents: Are They Reliable?* 5th ed., William B. Eerdmans Publishing Company, Grand Rapids, Michigan, 1960.

Budziszewski, J., *How to Stay Christian in College,* NavPress, Colorado Springs, 1999.

Chapman, Colin, *The Case for Christianity*, William B. Eerdmans Publishing Company, Grand Rapids, Michigan, 1981.

Craig, William Lane, *Apologetics: An Introduction.*, Moody Press, Chicago, 1984.

_____, *Reasonable Faith,* Crossway Books, Wheaton, Illinois, 1984.

Geisler, Norman L., *Christian Apologetics,* Baker Book House, Grand Rapids, Michigan, 1976

Geisler, Norman and Ron Brooks, *When Skeptics Ask,* Baker Books, Grand Rapids, Michigan, 1990.

Geisler, Norman and Thomas Howe, *When Critics Ask,* Victor Books, Wheaton, Illinois, 1992.

Glynn, Patrick, *God: The Evidence*, Three Rivers Press, 1999.

Greenleaf, Simon, *The Testimony of the Evangelists*, Kregel Classics, Grand Rapids, Michigan, 1995.

Habermas, Gary R., *The Resurrection of Jesus: An Apologetic,* Baker Book House, Grand Rapids, Michigan, 1980.

Hanegraaf, Hank, *Christianity in Crisis,* Harvest House, Eugene, Oregon, 1997.

*Hunt, Dave, *In Defense of the Faith.* Eugene, Oregon: Harvest House, 1996.

Kreeft, Peter and Ronald Tacelli, *Handbook of Christian Apologetics*, InterVarsity Press, Downer Groves, Illinois, 1994.

Laidlaw, Robert A., *The Reason Why,* Bridge Publishing, South Plainfield, New Jersey, 1994.

Lewis, C.S., *Mere Christianity,* Macmillan Publishing Company, New York, 1943.

_____, *Miracles: A Preliminary Study,* Macmillan Publishing Company, New York, 1947.

_____, *The Problem of Pain*, Macmillan Publishing Company, New York, 1962.

Little, Paul E., *Know Why You Believe*, InterVarsity Press, Downers Grove, Illinois, 1968.

Lutzer, Erwin, *Seven Reasons Why You Can Trust the Bible*, Moody Press, Chicago, 1998.

*McDowell, Josh, *Don't Check Your Brains at the Door*, An Interactive Video Series for Junior High and High School Students, Word Publishing, Irving, Texas, 1992.

*_____, *Evidence That Demands A Verdict*, vol. 1, Here's Life Publishers, San Bernardino, California, 1972.

_____, *More Than A Carpenter*, Tyndale House, Wheaton, Illinois, 1977.

_____, *The Resurrection Factor*, Here's Life Publishers, San Bernardino, California, 1977.

*McDowell, Josh and Bob Hostetler, *Don't Check Your Brains at the Door*, Word Publishing, Dallas, 1992.

*McDowell, Josh and Bill Wilson, *He Walked Among Us: Evidence for the Historical Jesus*, 1988 and Thomas Nelson Publishers, Nashville, 1993.

*McElveen, Floyd, *Evidence You Never Knew Existed*, Institute for Religious Research, Grand Rapids, Michigan, 1998.

McGrath, Alister E., *Explaining Your Faith Without Losing Your Friends*, Zondervan Publishing House, Grand Rapids, Michigan, 1989.

*Montgomery, John Warwick, Tapes Series "Contemporary Apologetics I."

_____, *Faith Founded on Fact*, Trinity Press, Newburgh, Indiana, 1978.

Morison, Frank, *Who Moved the Stone?* 1930 and Lamplighter Books, Grand Rapids, Michigan, 1958.

Morris, Henry M., *Many Infallible Proofs*, Creation-Life Publishers, San Diego, 1974.

Sire, James W., *The Universe Next Door*, InterVarsity Press, Downers Grove, Illinois, 1976.

_____, *Why Should Anyone Believe Anything At All?* InterVarsity Press, Downers Grove, Illinois, 1994.

*Sproul, R.C., *Reason to Believe*, Zondervan, Grand Rapids, Michigan, 1981.

*Story, Dan, *Engaging the Closed Minded*, Kregel Publications, Grand Rapids, Michigan, 1999.

*Strobel, Lee, *The Case for Christ*, Zondervan. Grand Rapids, Michigan, 1998.

Zacharias, Ravi, *Can Man Live Without God*, Word Publishing, Dallas, 1994.

ABOUT THE AUTHOR

Mark Bird has been teaching Apologetics, Systematic Theology, and Evangelism at God's Bible School and College (Cincinnati, Ohio) for close to 10 years. As Christian Service Director at GBS, he supervised several college outreach ministries. He received his M.A. in theology from Wesley Biblical Seminary and the D.Min. degree from Grace Theological Seminary, where his concentration was in Apologetics.

Dr. Bird has also written *How Can You Be Sure?: Charles Stanley and John Wesley Debate Salvation and Security*. He can be reached at MBird@gbs.edu with questions or comments. Mark resides in Cincinnati with his wife Kristin and two young daughters.